THE HASSLE-FREE MEDITERRANEAN DIET COOKBOOKFOR BEGINNERS

*Budget-Friendly, Delicious 15-Minute Recipes for Two
to Build a Healthier Lifestyle & Lose Weight
While Enjoying Your Favorite Foods*

Sophia Marino

For this book, we deliberately avoided using photographic paper by choosing eco-friendly paper to be as environmentally sustainable as possible

First Printing Edition, 2024
Printed in the United States of America
Available from Amazon.com and other retail outlets

INTRODUCTION

The Mediterranean diet is not just a set of meals; it's a way of life. Rooted in the traditions of countries like Greece, Italy, and Spain, this approach to eating focuses on whole, natural foods that are as flavorful as they are nourishing. For decades, people in these regions have enjoyed diets rich in fresh fruits, vegetables, whole grains, and healthy fats, all while savoring meals with family and friends.

What makes the Mediterranean diet truly unique is its balance. It's not about strict restrictions or cutting out entire food groups. Instead, it encourages eating a variety of nutrient-dense foods in moderation, allowing you to enjoy delicious meals without feeling deprived. The Mediterranean diet is more than just a tool for weight loss; it's a path to long-term health and well-being.

I can personally speak to its transformative power. Although I was raised in the United States, my family roots trace back to Italy, where food has always been a central part of life. Growing up, I adapted to the typical American way of eating—fast, convenient, and often processed. By the time I reached my 40s, I started feeling the effects. My energy levels were low, I had gained weight, and I was dealing with several chronic health issues, including high blood pressure, joint pain, and rising cholesterol levels. Despite my Italian heritage, I had strayed far from the traditional foods that my grandparents once ate, and it showed in my health.

Then, in my mid-40s, I made a life-changing decision. I moved to Greece for two years, and that's when everything shifted. Immersing myself in the local culture, I slowly began to adopt their way of eating—fresh, whole foods like vegetables, olive oil, lean proteins, and legumes. It wasn't an overnight transformation, but over time, I noticed significant improvements. My weight began to drop steadily, my high blood pressure stabilized without medication, and the chronic joint pain that had plagued me for years became more manageable. Even my cholesterol levels returned to a healthy range.

While living in Greece made it easier for me to embrace this new way of eating, anyone can do it. You don't have to move abroad to start feeling the benefits. Once you discover your own set of favorite recipes and learn how to prepare them, the transition becomes effortless. When you begin to experience how much better you feel, adapting to a Mediterranean lifestyle will feel natural. It's about finding the right balance of foods that work for you, and that's exactly what this cookbook aims to help you do.

During my time in Greece, I also had the chance to travel around Europe and fell in love with the bold flavors of Middle Eastern cuisine. The spices, the aromatic herbs, and the richness of dishes from places like Lebanon and Turkey captivated me. That's why you'll notice many recipes in this book have a little twist—

whether it's a touch of cumin or a sprinkle of sumac—bringing an extra layer of flavor and complexity. These additions elevate traditional Mediterranean meals to another level and create dishes that are both comforting and exciting.

Beyond just the physical health benefits, the Mediterranean diet taught me something even more valuable—it taught me how to nourish myself, not just eat for pleasure. In our modern world, we've become so accustomed to eating foods that are engineered to appeal to our senses, often loaded with salt, sugar, and fat to trigger cravings. We eat because something looks good, because it's quick, or because it's satisfying in the moment. But that's not what food is meant to be. Food is meant to nurture us, to give our bodies the energy and nutrients we need to thrive.

With this cookbook, I encourage you to focus on the nourishing value of the meals—the fresh ingredients, the balanced nutrients—and trust that this way of eating will satisfy you in a deeper, more meaningful way. It's about learning to listen to what your body needs, not just what your appetite wants in the moment.

The Mediterranean diet didn't just change the way I ate; it changed the way I lived. I began savoring meals, sitting down to eat with others, and appreciating the simplicity of fresh, seasonal ingredients. That's when I realized the power of this diet isn't just in the food—it's in the lifestyle.

Research supports these benefits. Numerous studies have shown that following a Mediterranean diet can reduce the risk of heart disease, stroke, and type 2 diabetes. The PREDIMED trial, for example, revealed that people who embraced the Mediterranean diet had significantly lower rates of cardiovascular disease compared to those following a low-fat diet.

This cookbook is here to help you bring that same joy and health into your own kitchen. With recipes that are quick, easy, and budget-friendly, we hope to show you that adopting a Mediterranean lifestyle doesn't have to be complicated or time-consuming. So, let's get started on this journey together toward healthier eating and living, one delicious meal at a time.

WHY THE MEDITERRANEAN DIET

The Mediterranean is a time-tested way of eating that has been associated with some of the best health outcomes in the world. At its core, this diet emphasizes a balance of whole, nutrient-dense foods that support overall well-being. The foundation of the Mediterranean diet lies in the variety of plant-based foods that make up the base of its food pyramid—fruits, vegetables, whole grains, and healthy fats like extra virgin olive oil. These foods, rich in fiber, antioxidants, and healthy fats, form the bedrock of everyday meals and have been shown to contribute to better heart health and longevity.

As you move up the Mediterranean food pyramid, you'll find moderate portions of fish, poultry, and dairy, which are consumed regularly but in smaller amounts. These lean proteins are essential for maintaining muscle health and supporting metabolism, and they bring a wealth of nutrients to the table. Red meats and sweets, in contrast, appear at the very top of the pyramid, meant to be enjoyed only occasionally, helping to prevent the overconsumption of saturated fats and sugars, both of which are linked to chronic conditions like heart disease and diabetes.

This way of eating is all about variety, balance, and moderation. The Mediterranean diet encourages you to enjoy your meals, savor the flavors, and focus on nourishing your body with every bite. Research from the New England Journal of Medicine has shown that this balanced approach can reduce the risk of cardiovascular disease by up to 30%. The combination of

healthy fats from olive oil and the fiber from vegetables and legumes works to lower inflammation, improve cholesterol levels, and support overall heart health.

When compared to the typical American food pyramid, the differences are striking. The American pyramid tends to emphasize grains—many of which are highly refined and processed—along with larger quantities of red meat and dairy. Processed foods and sugary snacks also play a prominent role in the modern American diet. Unfortunately, this way of eating has been linked to higher rates of obesity, heart disease, and diabetes, as the abundance of convenience foods often leads to overconsumption of empty calories and a lack of essential nutrients.

In contrast, the Mediterranean diet promotes whole, unprocessed foods that are nutrient-dense and naturally low in unhealthy fats. People who follow the Mediterranean diet tend to have lower rates of heart disease, obesity, and other chronic conditions. This isn't just about avoiding unhealthy foods—it's about choosing foods that actively support your health. The antioxidants in fruits and vegetables help reduce inflammation, the fiber promotes digestive health, and the healthy fats from olive oil protect your heart. All these factors combined contribute to a longer, healthier life.

ESSENTIAL MEDITERRANEAN PANTRY

One of the keys to success with the Mediterranean diet is having a well-stocked pantry filled with wholesome, versatile ingredients that can form the foundation of countless meals. By focusing on high-quality staples, you'll find that preparing Mediterranean dishes becomes second nature. Here are some of the essential items that will help you create nourishing, delicious meals that align with this way of eating.

EXTRA VIRGIN OLIVE OIL

At the heart of the Mediterranean diet is extra virgin olive oil, a staple in nearly every meal. It's used for cooking, drizzling over salads, and adding flavor to a wide variety of dishes. More than just a flavorful addition, extra virgin olive oil is incredibly beneficial for your health. Rich in monounsaturated fats and antioxidants like polyphenols, olive oil has been shown to reduce inflammation and lower cholesterol levels. These benefits contribute to better heart health and lower rates of cardiovascular disease, making it one of the healthiest fats you can incorporate into your diet. Studies consistently show that people who consume olive oil regularly have a reduced risk of heart disease and stroke.

WHOLE GRAINS

Whole grains like quinoa, bulgur, and farro are fundamental to the Mediterranean diet. These grains are rich in fiber, vitamins, and minerals, providing slow-digesting carbohydrates that help sustain energy levels throughout the day. Unlike refined grains, which are stripped of their nutrients, whole grains maintain their fiber content, promoting digestive health and helping to regulate blood sugar levels. Including whole grains in your meals supports a steady, balanced source of energy and can help reduce the risk of developing type 2 diabetes. Research has shown that a diet rich in whole grains is associated with a lower risk of heart disease.

LEGUMES

Legumes, such as chickpeas, lentils, and beans, are a staple in Mediterranean cooking. They're incredibly versatile and are often used in soups, salads, and spreads like hummus. Legumes are a fantastic plant-based source of protein and fiber, making them both filling and nutritious. The high fiber content promotes gut health and aids in managing blood sugar levels, helping to prevent spikes and crashes in energy. In fact, the American Heart Association has found that regular consumption of legumes can improve heart health by lowering blood pressure and cholesterol levels.

NUTS, SEEDS, AND TAHINI

Nuts and seeds, including almonds, walnuts, flaxseeds, and sesame seeds, are frequently used as snacks or added to dishes for a satisfying crunch. These nutrient-dense foods are packed with healthy fats, fiber, and essential vitamins and minerals. A particularly popular ingredient in Mediterranean cooking is tahini, a creamy paste made from ground sesame seeds. Tahini is rich in healthy fats, protein, and minerals like calcium and magnesium, which support bone health and provide an excellent source of plant-based nutrition.

Studies from Harvard University have shown that a diet rich in nuts and seeds is linked to a lower risk of cardiovascular disease. The combination of healthy fats and fiber in these foods helps reduce inflammation and supports heart health. Whether used in spreads like hummus, drizzled on salads, or as a base for sauces, tahini adds a rich, nutty flavor to Mediterranean dishes while contributing valuable nutrients.

FRESH HERBS

Fresh herbs like parsley, basil, and oregano are used generously in Mediterranean cooking, not just for flavor, but also for their health benefits. Herbs are loaded with antioxidants and have anti-inflammatory properties, which can support overall health. Incorporating fresh herbs into your meals is an easy way to boost both the flavor and the nutritional value of your dishes without relying on added salt or unhealthy fats.

ANTIOXIDANT HERBS & SPICE MIXES

Herbs and spices are at the heart of Mediterranean cooking. Not only do they add vibrant flavors to dishes, but they also come packed with powerful antioxidants that help protect your body from oxidative stress and inflammation. Here's a look at some of the most commonly used antioxidant-rich herbs in the Mediterranean diet, along with a simple spice mix you can use to enhance your meals.

KEY ANTIOXIDANT HERBS AND THEIR BENEFITS

BASIL

- Benefits: Rich in antioxidants like eugenol and flavonoids, basil helps reduce inflammation and combat free radicals in the body. It also has antibacterial properties and supports digestion.
- Best for: Salads, pesto, tomato-based dishes, and sauces. It pairs wonderfully with vegetables, pasta, and fish.

OREGANO

- Benefits: Oregano is packed with phenolic compounds, which have been shown to have antimicrobial and antioxidant effects. It also supports respiratory health and has anti-inflammatory properties.
- Best for: Meat dishes like chicken or lamb, as well as marinades, roasted vegetables, and pizza toppings.

ROSEMARY

- Benefits: Known for its high levels of rosmarinic acid, rosemary has strong antioxidant and anti-inflammatory effects. It's also great for improving digestion and cognitive function.
- Best for: Grilled meats like lamb or chicken, roasted potatoes, and fish. It pairs especially well with hearty and roasted dishes.

THYME

- Benefits: Thyme contains thymol, a powerful antioxidant and antimicrobial agent that promotes respiratory health and reduces inflammation. It also supports immune function.
- Best for: Vegetable stews, soups, roasted vegetables, and meat marinades. Thyme is versatile and enhances both light and hearty dishes.

PARSLEY

- Benefits: Parsley is rich in vitamins A, C, and K, and its antioxidant compounds help detoxify the body. It also supports kidney function and bone health.
- Best for: Fish dishes, salads, tabbouleh, and grain bowls. Parsley adds a fresh, bright flavor to almost any dish.

CUMIN

- Benefits: Cumin is packed with antioxidants and has been shown to improve digestion, reduce inflammation, and regulate blood sugar levels. It's also known for its antibacterial properties.
- Best for: Meats like beef or lamb, as well as lentils and vegetable stews. It's also a great spice for Middle Eastern-inspired dishes.

CORIANDER

- Benefits: Coriander seeds are rich in antioxidants, including quercetin, which has anti-inflammatory and immune-boosting properties. It also aids in digestion and promotes heart health.
- Best for: Spice rubs for fish and chicken, soups, and vegetable curries. It adds warmth and depth to dishes.

TURMERIC

- Benefits: Turmeric contains curcumin, a potent antioxidant and anti-inflammatory compound that is well-known for its ability to improve joint health and reduce inflammation in the body.
- Best for: Vegetable dishes, soups, and curries. Turmeric is especially good for adding warmth and color to grain bowls and roasted vegetables.

SIMPLE ANTIOXIDANT SPICE MIX

Here's 5 versatile antioxidant-rich spice mixes that you can create at home to elevate the flavors of your dishes. You can store them in airtight containers in a cool, dark place. They'll stay fresh for up to 3 months, allowing you to have flavorful blends on hand whenever you need them.

- **ZESTY HERB BLEND**

Best for: Fish and Chicken

- 2 tablespoons dried oregano
- 2 tablespoons dried thyme
- 1 tablespoon lemon zest (dried or fresh)
- 1 tablespoon dried basil
- 1 teaspoon garlic powder
- 1 teaspoon sea salt
- ½ teaspoon black pepper

How to use: This zesty mix is perfect for fish and chicken dishes. Rub it onto salmon or white fish before grilling, or marinate chicken with olive oil and the spice mix for a bright, citrusy flavor. You can also use it as a finishing sprinkle over salads or grain bowls.

SMOKY PAPRIKA SPICE MIX

Best for: Meat and Vegetables

- 1 tablespoon smoked paprika
- 1 tablespoon ground cumin
- 1 tablespoon dried rosemary
- 1 tablespoon garlic powder
- 1 teaspoon ground black pepper
- 1 teaspoon cayenne pepper (optional, for heat)

How to use: Ideal for roasted meats like lamb or beef, this smoky mix adds depth and warmth. Coat meat with this spice mix before roasting or grilling. It's also great for sprinkling over roasted vegetables like sweet potatoes, carrots, or bell peppers to give them a smoky, slightly spicy kick.

LEMONY SUMAC SPICE MIX

Best for: Vegetables, Fish, and Grains

- 1 tablespoon sumac (for a tangy, lemon-like flavor)
- 1 tablespoon ground coriander
- 1 tablespoon dried parsley
- 1 teaspoon ground cumin
- 1 teaspoon garlic powder
- ½ teaspoon sea salt

How to use: This fresh, tangy mix works wonders with roasted vegetables, grilled fish, or mixed into grain salads like tabbouleh or couscous. The sumac adds a lemony brightness that enhances the flavors of fresh dishes, making it perfect for a light and zesty touch.

MEDITERRANEAN WARM SPICE MIX

Best for: Lamb, Beef, and Stews

- 2 tablespoons ground cumin
- 1 tablespoon ground cinnamon
- 1 tablespoon ground coriander
- 1 tablespoon ground allspice
- 1 teaspoon ground cloves
- 1 teaspoon black pepper

How to use: This warm, earthy spice mix is ideal for lamb or beef stews, Mediterranean-style meatballs, or kebabs. The combination of cumin, cinnamon, and cloves adds a deep, aromatic flavor that pairs beautifully with slow-cooked dishes. Try using this mix as a rub for lamb chops or in a hearty lentil stew for a bold, comforting flavor profile.

HERBY GARLIC MIX

Best for: Chicken, Fish, and Grains

- 2 tablespoons dried oregano
- 1 tablespoon dried basil
- 1 tablespoon dried thyme
- 1 tablespoon garlic powder
- 1 teaspoon sea salt
- 1 teaspoon black pepper

How to use: This versatile garlic-infused herb mix is perfect for seasoning chicken or fish before grilling or baking. It also works well sprinkled over roasted vegetables or stirred into grain dishes like quinoa or bulgur. The classic Mediterranean herbs and garlic blend bring out the best in almost any dish.

BALANCED WEEKLY GUIDE

The Mediterranean diet is all about balance, moderation, and enjoying a wide variety of nutrient-dense foods. To help you integrate this lifestyle seamlessly into your routine, we've created a practical weekly guide on how often to include key foods like vegetables, whole grains, fish, eggs, and even red meat.

This guide is not rigid—it's flexible enough to adapt to your personal tastes and what's available to you each week. The key to success is variety, portion control, and most importantly, savoring the food you eat.

WEEKLY BREAKDOWN FOR MEDITERRANEAN DIET

Vegetables: At every meal (daily) - Aim for half of your plate to be vegetables (raw or cooked)

Fruits: 2-3 times daily   - 1 medium-sized fruit or 1 cup of berries per serving

Whole Grains: At most meals (daily)   - 1 serving = ½ cup cooked grains like quinoa, bulgur, or whole wheat

Legumes: 3-4 times per week   1 serving = 1 cup cooked lentils, beans, or chickpeas

Fish: 2-3 times per week - 1 serving = 3-4 oz of fatty fish like salmon, sardines, or mackerel

Poultry (white meat): 2 times per week - 1 serving = 3-4 oz chicken or turkey

Eggs: Up to 4 times per week- 1-2 eggs per serving

Dairy (yogurt, cheese): 1-2 times per day- 1 serving = 1 cup yogurt or 1 oz cheese

Nuts and Seeds: Daily   1 serving - a handful (about 1 oz)

Red Meat: Up to 1-2 times per month - 1 serving = 3-4 oz

Olive Oil: Daily (used for cooking or drizzling) - 1-2 tablespoons per meal

Wine (optional): In moderation (up to 1 glass per day) - 5 oz of red wine (optional, during meals)

Sweets: Limited (small portions, a few times a week - Preferably homemade using natural ingredients like honey

PRACTICAL TIPS FOR MED. EATING

To make following this guide easier, here are some practical tips you can incorporate into your routine to help plan meals, save time, and keep costs down.

MEAL PLANNING TIPS

Batch Cooking: Prepare whole grains like quinoa, bulgur, or farro, and legumes like chickpeas or lentils in bulk at the start of the week. This makes it easy to throw together quick meals without a lot of prep work.

Meal Prep Ideas: Pre-chop vegetables and store them in airtight containers to have ready-to-go ingredients for salads, stir-fries, and snacks. This can help you stay consistent with your vegetable intake and reduce cooking time.

Freezing Fish: Fresh fish can be expensive and has a short shelf life, so buy fresh and freeze portions. This ensures you have fish available to meet the 2-3 times per week recommendation.

2. PORTION CONTROL

When building meals, try to make half of your plate vegetables, a quarter whole grains, and a quarter lean protein (like fish, chicken, or legumes). This keeps your meals balanced and nutrient-dense. Remember that the Mediterranean diet focuses on quality over quantity when it comes to protein, especially red meat and poultry. Aim for smaller portions and pair them with a variety of plant-based sides.

3. SMART SNACKING

Healthy Mediterranean snacks include raw vegetables with hummus, a handful of nuts, or fruit with a bit of cheese. These nutrient-dense snacks help stabilize blood sugar levels and provide lasting energy throughout the day.

Practice mindful snacking by avoiding distractions like phones or TVs during meals. This helps you tune into your hunger and fullness signals.

4. HYDRATION MATTERS

Water is the best beverage for hydration. Try to drink water throughout the day, and opt for herbal teas if you want variety. Limiting sugary drinks or sodas is key in following the Mediterranean diet's emphasis on natural, unprocessed ingredients. For those who enjoy wine, limit it to 1 glass per day with a meal, following the traditional Mediterranean practice of enjoying it in moderation.

5. STAY FLEXIBLE

Some weeks, you may find it harder to include certain ingredients, like fresh fish or specific fruits and vegetables. That's okay! Flexibility is part of the Mediterranean lifestyle. Do your best to meet the general guidelines, but don't stress if you can't adhere to them perfectly every week. Use canned or frozen fish and vegetables as convenient alternatives when fresh options aren't available. Canned tomatoes and beans, for example, are staples in Mediterranean cooking and are cost-effective.

6. EMBRACE SEASONAL EATING

Eating seasonally not only helps you get fresher produce but also reduces costs. Check your local farmers' markets or grocery stores to find what's in season, and let those ingredients inspire your meals. Seasonal produce is also more flavorful and nutrient-dense.

Plan your meals around what's in season: tomatoes, peppers, and zucchini in the summer, and root vegetables, squash, and leafy greens in the cooler months.

7. MASTER SIMPLE COOKING TECHNIQUES

Roasting is a great way to bring out the natural flavors of vegetables. Toss them in olive oil, sprinkle with herbs, and roast for a healthy, delicious side dish. Learn to make your own salad dressings using olive oil, lemon juice, and fresh herbs. This eliminates the need for store-bought dressings that often contain unnecessary additives. Use herbs and spices liberally to enhance flavor without relying on too much salt. Basil, oregano, cumin, and paprika are commonly used in Mediterranean cooking and add complexity to simple dishes.

A LIFESTYLE, NOT A DIET

Above all, remember that the Mediterranean diet is more than just a way of eating—it's a lifestyle. It's about enjoying food in a relaxed, mindful way, sharing meals with loved ones, and incorporating regular physical activity into your day. Don't aim for perfection; aim for balance. Over time, this approach will nourish your body, improve your health, and enrich your life.

Unlike many restrictive diets, the Mediterranean way of eating isn't about what you can't have; it's about celebrating what you can. The diet encourages you to eat a variety of nutrient-dense foods like fruits, vegetables, legumes, and whole grains. Meals are often shared with family and friends, creating an atmosphere of connection and joy. In fact, food is seen as a way to bring people together, and these social meals have a powerful impact on emotional and physical health.

Another key aspect of this lifestyle is its focus on moderation. For instance, while the diet promotes frequent consumption of plant-based foods, it recommends limiting certain foods to specific occasions. Red meat, for example, is eaten only a few times a month, helping reduce the intake of unhealthy fats. Eggs can be enjoyed up to four times a week, and poultry or fish is encouraged a few times per week for lean, nutrient-rich protein. This balance allows for indulgence without excess, helping maintain a healthy, sustainable approach to eating.

Whether it's the moderate consumption of red wine with meals or the careful balance of indulgence and health, the Mediterranean diet teaches you to eat mindfully. You're encouraged to listen to your body, eating until satisfied, not stuffed. This mindful approach to eating promotes a healthier relationship with food and

discourages the cycles of overeating that are common in many modern diets. This approach extends beyond food. Daily movement is a natural part of life in Mediterranean cultures. Whether it's walking to the market, working in the garden, or engaging in light physical activity, the Mediterranean lifestyle seamlessly integrates exercise into everyday life. Combined with a diet rich in antioxidants, healthy fats, and fiber, this active lifestyle contributes to the prevention of chronic diseases like heart disease, diabetes, and even some forms of cancer.

The benefits of the Mediterranean lifestyle are backed by science. Studies show that this way of living contributes to lower rates of depression and cognitive decline, thanks in part to the strong social connections and daily physical activity that are woven into Mediterranean culture. Research on Blue Zones—regions around the world where people live longer and healthier lives—has repeatedly highlighted the importance of these lifestyle factors. In many of these areas, like the island of Ikaria in Greece, people live well into their 90s or even 100s, enjoying long lives that are both physically and mentally healthy.

BUDGET-FRIENDLY MED. EATING

One of the common misconceptions about the Mediterranean diet is that it's expensive to follow. However, with a few practical strategies, you can enjoy all the benefits of this healthy way of eating without breaking the bank. In fact, many of the staples of the Mediterranean diet—grains, legumes, and seasonal vegetables—are among the most affordable foods you can buy.

In the U.S., finding fresh, affordable food can sometimes feel like a challenge, but with a little planning, it's entirely possible. One of the best ways to save money while sticking to the Mediterranean diet is to explore various shopping options. Local farmers' markets are a fantastic place to start, offering fresh, seasonal produce that is often cheaper than supermarket options. Plus, shopping at farmers' markets means you're supporting local farmers while getting fruits and vegetables at their peak flavor and nutrition. As produce reaches the end of its season, prices often drop, allowing for great deals on larger quantities. Grocery chains such as Aldi, Trader Joe's, and Walmart are also excellent for affordable organic and fresh produce. Many of these stores offer loyalty programs or mobile apps that provide additional savings through coupons or rewards. Don't overlook wholesale stores like Costco or Sam's Club, where you can buy pantry staples—grains, legumes, olive oil—in bulk at a lower cost per unit. This makes it easier to stock up on Mediterranean essentials without overspending. Another great option for fresh produce is subscribing to a Community Supported Agriculture (CSA) program. With a CSA, you pay a set amount upfront and receive weekly or bi-weekly boxes of seasonal produce directly from local farms, saving both money and time spent grocery shopping.

While shopping smart is key, another important aspect of saving money with the Mediterranean diet is eating out less frequently. The cost of dining at restaurants, especially those offering Mediterranean-inspired dishes, can quickly add up. Cooking at home allows you to enjoy the same rich flavors without the hefty price tag. You also gain control over ingredients, portion sizes, and nutritional quality. By focusing on simple, fresh ingredients, you can recreate restaurant-quality meals for a fraction of the cost.

One of the easiest ways to keep costs low is to buy grains like quinoa, bulgur, and whole wheat pasta, as well as legumes like chickpeas and lentils, in bulk. These pantry staples are affordable, versatile, and can form the foundation of a wide variety of meals—from hearty stews to fresh salads. Another great money-saving tip is to plan your meals around what's in season. Seasonal fruits and vegetables are not only more flavorful, but they are also typically more affordable. Grocery stores and farmers' markets often have special deals on produce that's at its peak, making it easy to build nutrient-rich meals around what's available.

If fresh ingredients are out of reach, canned or frozen options can be just as nutritious and cost-effective. Canned tomatoes, for instance, are a staple in many Mediterranean dishes and offer a convenient way to add flavor and nutrition to your meals without breaking the bank. Similarly, canned or frozen fish like sardines and salmon are excellent sources of heart-healthy omega-3 fatty acids, providing an affordable alternative to fresh seafood. For many, some healthy foods commonly associated with the Mediterranean diet—like avocados, certain types of fish, and nuts—can be on the pricier side. Fortunately, there are plenty of affordable substitutions that offer similar nutritional benefits. For example: Instead of avocado, which can be expensive, you can use hummus or tahini to add healthy fats and creamy texture to your meals. Both are rich in healthy fats, fiber, and nutrients while being more budget-friendly.

Sardines or canned mackerel are excellent, cheaper alternatives to more expensive fish like fresh salmon. Both are high in omega-3 fatty acids and provide the same heart-healthy benefits at a fraction of the cost.

Sunflower seeds are a fantastic, affordable substitute for pine nuts in salads or pestos. They still provide a crunchy texture and healthy fats but are far more budget-conscious.

Frozen berries are a great alternative to fresh berries when they're out of season. They retain their nutritional value and are typically much cheaper than fresh berries.

Frozen spinach can be used in place of fresh spinach, saving you money while still providing the same rich iron and vitamin content. It's also an easy way to reduce food waste, as frozen veggies last longer.

Canned beans are a great, budget-friendly substitute for fresh or dried beans, providing the same fiber and protein with less prep time and often at a lower cost.

Sweet potatoes are an excellent substitute for more expensive starches like butternut squash. They provide a similar texture and nutrient profile, offering plenty of fiber, vitamins A and C, and are more wallet-friendly.

Plain Greek yogurt can be a cheaper alternative to higher-priced dairy options like ricotta or mascarpone. It's versatile and can be used in savory dishes, smoothies, or even as a base for creamy sauces.

Carrots or parsnips can be substituted for asparagus or artichokes in recipes, especially when those vegetables are out of season or particularly pricey.

Another way to keep your budget in check while eating healthily is to incorporate more plant-based meals. Research has shown that plant-based diets, which focus on grains, legumes, and vegetables, are significantly more affordable than diets high in meat and processed foods. By relying on plant-based proteins, you not only save money but also reduce your intake of unhealthy fats and preservatives, supporting long-term health goals. Studies from the Journal of Hunger & Environmental Nutrition confirm that plant-based diets stretch your grocery budget while delivering the nutrients your body needs to thrive.

With a little creativity and mindful shopping, it's clear that the Mediterranean diet can be both affordable and accessible, providing you with delicious, nutrient-dense meals that won't break the bank.

WHY THIS COOKBOOK?

The Mediterranean diet is known for its incredible health benefits, but many people feel overwhelmed by the idea of incorporating its principles into their busy lives. That's where this cookbook comes in. We've designed this collection of recipes specifically for you, focusing on quick, budget-friendly meals that are easy to prepare and perfectly portioned for smaller households.

SIMPLIFIED FOR BUSY LIFESTYLES

In today's fast-paced world, spending hours in the kitchen is often not an option. That's why this cookbook simplifies traditional Mediterranean recipes into meals that can be prepared in just 15-20 minutes using common ingredients you can easily find in your local grocery store. From breakfasts that energize your morning to quick 15-minute feasts and hearty sides, each recipe is designed to fit seamlessly into your busy schedule without sacrificing flavor or nutrition.

PORTION-CONTROLLED FOR TWO

One of the unique features of this cookbook is its focus on portion control. The recipes are tailored for two people, making them ideal for singles, couples, or even small families who want to avoid food waste while still enjoying a variety of meals. Research shows that portion control is a critical factor in maintaining a healthy weight. The Mediterranean diet naturally supports this by focusing on nutrient-dense, satisfying foods like vegetables, legumes, and lean proteins. These ingredients provide the necessary nutrients while keeping calorie intake in check, helping you feel full and nourished without overeating.

MEAL PLANNING AND BATCH-COOKING FOR CONVENIENCE

We encourage readers to experiment with meal planning and batch-cooking, strategies that not only save time but also help maintain a consistent, healthy diet. By preparing meals in advance or cooking larger batches to enjoy throughout the week, you reduce the temptation to rely on processed or fast foods during busy days. Studies have shown that people who plan their meals are more likely to stick to healthy eating habits. Meal planning also allows for better portion control, helping you maintain a balanced diet that supports your long-term health goals.

SUPPORTING HEALTHY WEIGHT MAINTENANCE

This cookbook also naturally supports weight loss and healthy weight maintenance. By focusing on whole, nutrient-dense foods like vegetables, whole grains, and healthy fats, these recipes help you manage hunger while preventing overeating. The Mediterranean diet is rich in fiber and healthy fats, two components that are key to long-term weight loss success. Fiber, found in vegetables, legumes, and whole grains, helps slow digestion, keeping you full longer. Healthy fats from sources like olive oil and nuts are both satiating and nourishing, giving your body the energy it needs without the excess calories.

In fact, research from the American Journal of Clinical Nutrition has found that people following a Mediterranean diet are more successful at maintaining weight loss over the long term compared to those on low-fat diets. The balanced approach of the Mediterranean diet—focusing on the right types of fats and carbohydrates—provides a more sustainable way to lose weight and keep it off, without feeling deprived.

This cookbook is here to make the Mediterranean diet accessible, enjoyable, and practical for your everyday life. Whether you're new to this way of eating or simply looking for ways to streamline your meals, the recipes in this book are designed to meet your needs. By incorporating meal planning, portion control, and quick-prep meals, you can enjoy all the benefits of the Mediterranean diet without the hassle.

BREAKFAST

ZA'ATAR SCRAMBLED EGGS WITH FETA & AVOCADO

PREP TIME: 10 MINUTES
DIETARY: Dairy-free option

'80 CALORIES, 15G PROTEIN, 12G CARBS, 22G FAT

INGREDIENTS:
- 4 eggs
- 1 tbsp olive oil
- 2 tbsp crumbled feta (optional)
- 1 tsp za'atar (or rosemary)
- ½ avocado (sliced)
- Salt and pepper to taste

INSTRUCTIONS:
1. Heat olive oil in a pan over medium heat.
2. Crack eggs into a bowl, season with salt, pepper, and za'atar, and whisk together.
3. Pour the eggs into the pan and cook, stirring gently, until softly scrambled (about 3-4 minutes).
4. Remove from heat and fold in crumbled feta if using.
5. Serve with sliced avocado on the side.

DAIRY-FREE: Omit the feta or use a dairy-free cheese alternative.

BATCH-COOKING SUGGESTION: Scrambled eggs don't store well, but you can prep the avocado slices and mix the za'atar with olive oil the night before to speed up the process in the morning.

GREEK YOGURT WITH HONEY-ROASTED FIGS & WALNUTS

PREP TIME: 10 MINUTES
DIETARY: Dairy-free option, vegan option

320 CALORIES, 12G PROTEIN, 30G CARBS, 18G FAT

INGREDIENTS:
- 1 cup Greek yogurt (or dairy-free yogurt)
- 4 fresh figs (halved)
- 1 tbsp honey (or maple syrup for vegan)
- 2 tbsp walnuts (chopped)
- 1 tbsp olive oil

INSTRUCTIONS:
1. Preheat the oven to 375°F (190°C).
2. Drizzle the figs with olive oil and roast for 8 minutes, until soft and caramelized.
3. Spoon Greek yogurt into a bowl, top with honey-roasted figs, and sprinkle with chopped walnuts.
4. Drizzle with honey and serve.

DAIRY-FREE: Use almond or coconut yogurt.
VEGAN: Replace honey with maple syrup or agave nectar.

BATCH-COOKING SUGGESTION: You can roast the figs ahead of time and store them in an airtight container. Add them to yogurt when ready to serve.

AVOCADO TOAST WITH WITH HERBED LABNEH & ROASTED CHICKPEAS

PREP TIME: 15 MINUTES
DIETARY: Gluten-free option, dairy-free option

350 CALORIES, 10G PROTEIN, 30G CARBS, 25G FAT

INGREDIENTS:

- 2 slices whole grain bread (or gluten-free bread)
- 1 ripe avocado (mashed)
- ¼ cup labneh (or Greek yogurt, or dairy-free yogurt for vegan)
- ½ cup canned chickpeas (rinsed and drained)
- 1 tsp cumin
- 1 tsp smoked paprika
- 1 tbsp olive oil
- ½ tsp za'atar or dried thyme
- Salt and pepper to taste
- Fresh parsley for garnish

INSTRUCTIONS:

1. Preheat the oven to 400°F (200°C). Toss the chickpeas with olive oil, cumin, smoked paprika, salt, and pepper. Roast for 12-15 minutes, until crispy.
2. While the chickpeas are roasting, mash the avocado in a bowl and season with salt and pepper.
3. Mix labneh with za'atar or dried thyme, and a pinch of salt.
4. Toast the bread slices. Spread each slice with the herbed labneh, followed by mashed avocado.
5. Top with roasted chickpeas and garnish with fresh parsley.
6. Drizzle with a little more olive oil and a pinch of smoked paprika before serving.

GLUTEN-FREE: Use gluten-free bread.
DAIRY-FREE: Use dairy-free yogurt or hummus instead of labneh.

BATCH-COOKING SUGGESTION: Make a big batch of roasted chickpeas and store them for up to 3 days. They're perfect as a topping for toast, salads, or as a snack.

LEFTOVER MAKEOVER: Any leftover avocado spread or labneh can be used as a dip for veggies or added to wraps for lunch.

SPINACH & FETA BREAKFAST WRAP

PREP TIME: 10 MINUTES
DIETARY: Gluten-free option, dairy-free option

290 CALORIES, 14G PROTEIN, 25G CARBS, 15G FAT

INGREDIENTS:

- 2 large eggs
- 1 tbsp olive oil
- ½ cup fresh spinach
- 2 tbsp crumbled feta
- 2 whole wheat tortillas (or gluten-free tortillas)
- Salt and pepper to taste

INSTRUCTIONS:

1. Heat olive oil in a pan over medium heat.
2. Crack eggs into the pan and scramble, then add fresh spinach and cook until wilted (about 2 minutes).
3. Remove from heat and fold in crumbled feta.
4. Warm the tortillas, fill each one with the scrambled egg and spinach mixture, then wrap tightly.
5. Serve immediately.

GLUTEN-FREE: Use gluten-free tortillas.
DAIRY-FREE: Omit feta or use a dairy-free cheese.

BATCH-COOKING SUGGESTION: Make extra wraps and store them in the fridge for up to 2 days. You can quickly reheat them in a pan or microwave.

MEDITERRANEAN BREAKFAST QUINOA BOWL

PREP TIME: 15 MINUTES
DIETARY: Gluten-free, dairy-free option, vegan option

350 CALORIES, 13G PROTEIN, 50G CARBS, 10G FAT

INGREDIENTS:

- ½ cup quinoa
- 1 tbsp olive oil
- 1 small cucumber (chopped)
- 1 small tomato (chopped)
- ¼ cup Kalamata olives (pitted and sliced)
- 2 tbsp crumbled feta (optional)
- Juice of 1 lemon
- Salt and pepper to taste

INSTRUCTIONS:

1. Cook quinoa according to package instructions and let cool slightly.
2. In a bowl, combine the cooked quinoa with chopped cucumber, tomato, olives, and olive oil.
3. Squeeze lemon juice over the mixture and season with salt and pepper.
4. Top with crumbled feta (optional) and serve.

DAIRY-FREE: Omit the feta or use a plant-based alternative.
VEGAN: Omit the feta for a fully vegan dish.

BATCH-COOKING SUGGESTION: Cook a larger batch of quinoa to use in other meals. This breakfast bowl can also be prepped ahead of time and stored in the fridge for up to 3 days.

TAHINI BANANA SMOOTHIE

PREP TIME: 5 MINUTES
DIETARY: Dairy-free, vegan, gluten-free

240 CALORIES, 5G PROTEIN, 35G CARBS, 10G FAT

INGREDIENTS:

- 1 banana
- 1 tbsp tahini
- 1 cup almond milk (or other plant-based milk)
- 1 tbsp honey (or maple syrup for vegan)
- ¼ tsp cinnamon

INSTRUCTIONS:

1. Combine all ingredients in a blender.
2. Blend until smooth and creamy.
3. Pour into a glass and enjoy.

BATCH-COOKING SUGGESTION: Prep the ingredients the night before by slicing the banana and keeping it in the fridge for a quick morning smoothie.

TOMATO & HERB OMELETTE

PREP TIME: 12 MINUTES
DIETARY: Dairy-free, gluten-free

220 CALORIES, 14G PROTEIN, 6G CARBS, 16G FAT

INGREDIENTS:

- 3 eggs
- 1 tbsp olive oil
- 1 medium tomato (diced)
- 1 tbsp fresh parsley (chopped)
- Salt and pepper to taste

INSTRUCTIONS:

1. Whisk the eggs in a bowl and season with salt and pepper.
2. Heat olive oil in a non-stick pan over medium heat.
3. Pour in the eggs and cook for 2-3 minutes. Add diced tomato and parsley to one side of the omelette.
4. Fold the omelette in half and cook for an additional 2-3 minutes.
5. Serve hot.

BATCH-COOKING SUGGESTION: Omelettes are best made fresh, but you can prep the tomatoes and herbs ahead of time to speed up the cooking process in the morning.

OLIVE OIL & LEMON ZEST MUFFINS

PREP TIME: 15 MINUTES
DIETARY: Gluten-free option, dairy-free

210 CALORIES, 5G PROTEIN, 28G CARBS, 10G FAT

INGREDIENTS:
- 1 cup flour (or gluten-free flour)
- ¼ cup olive oil
- ¼ cup almond milk (or other plant-based milk)
- 1 egg
- Zest of 1 lemon
- 1 tbsp honey
- 1 tsp baking powder

INSTRUCTIONS:
1. Preheat the oven to 350°F (175°C).
2. In a bowl, whisk together olive oil, almond milk, egg, lemon zest, and honey.
3. Add flour and baking powder, then stir until just combined.
4. Pour the batter into muffin tins and bake for 12-15 minutes, until a toothpick comes out clean.
5. Let cool before serving.

GLUTEN-FREE: Use gluten-free flour.
DAIRY-FREE: Use almond or plant-based milk.

BATCH-COOKING SUGGESTION: Bake a batch of muffins and store them for up to 4 days for a quick breakfast throughout the week.

TZATZIKI & CUCUMBER TOAST

PREP TIME: 10 MINUTES
DIETARY: Gluten-free option, dairy-free option

180 CALORIES, 7G PROTEIN, 20G CARBS, 8G FAT

INGREDIENTS:
- 2 slices whole grain bread (or gluten-free bread)
- ½ cup Greek yogurt (or dairy-free yogurt)
- ½ cucumber (sliced)
- 1 garlic clove (minced)
- 1 tbsp fresh dill (chopped)
- Salt and pepper to taste

INSTRUCTIONS:
1. Toast the bread and set aside.
2. Mix Greek yogurt with garlic, dill, salt, and pepper to make tzatziki.
3. Spread tzatziki on the toasted bread and top with cucumber slices.
4. Serve immediately.

GLUTEN-FREE: Use gluten-free bread.
DAIRY-FREE: Use dairy-free yogurt for the tzatziki

LEFTOVER MAKEOVER: Leftover tzatziki can be used as a dip or a sauce for sandwiches or wraps.

MEDITERRANEAN VEGGIE BREAKFAST SANDWICH

PREP TIME: 12 MINUTES
DIETARY: Gluten-free option, dairy-free option

350 CALORIES, 14G PROTEIN, 30G CARBS, 15G FAT

INGREDIENTS:
- 2 whole grain sandwich rolls (or gluten-free rolls)

- 1 tbsp olive oil
- ½ cup spinach (sautéed)
- 1 tomato (sliced)
- 2 eggs (fried)
- 2 tbsp hummus

INSTRUCTIONS:

1. Toast the sandwich rolls.
2. In a pan, heat olive oil and sauté spinach for 2 minutes.
3. Fry the eggs to your liking.
4. Spread hummus on each sandwich roll, add spinach, tomato, and the fried egg.
5. Serve warm.

GLUTEN-FREE: Use gluten-free rolls.
DAIRY-FREE: Naturally dairy-free.

BATCH-COOKING SUGGESTION: Sauté extra spinach and store it for later to quickly assemble sandwiches during the week.

BAKED EGGS WITH SPINACH & TOMATOES

PREP TIME: 15 MINUTES
DIETARY: Gluten-free, dairy-free

280 CALORIES, 12G PROTEIN, 10G CARBS, 18G FAT

INGREDIENTS:

- 4 eggs
- 1 tbsp olive oil
- 1 cup fresh spinach
- 1 medium tomato (diced)
- Salt and pepper to taste

INSTRUCTIONS:

1. Preheat oven to 375°F (190°C).
2. Heat olive oil in a pan and sauté spinach until wilted.
3. Place the spinach and diced tomato into a small ovenproof dish.
4. Crack eggs over the vegetables and season with salt and pepper.
5. Bake for 10-12 minutes, until the eggs are set.
6. Serve hot.

BATCH-COOKING SUGGESTION: Make a larger batch of baked eggs for a quick breakfast over the next few days.

CHIA PUDDING WITH ALMONDS & BERRIES

PREP TIME: 5 MINUTES (PLUS OVERNIGHT CHILLING)
DIETARY: Gluten-free, dairy-free, vegan

260 CALORIES, 8G PROTEIN, 25G CARBS, 15G FAT

INGREDIENTS:

- 2 tbsp chia seeds
- 1 cup almond milk (or any plant-based milk)
- 1 tbsp honey or maple syrup (for vegan)
- ¼ cup mixed berries
- 2 tbsp sliced almonds

INSTRUCTIONS:

1. In a bowl or jar, mix chia seeds, almond milk, and honey. Stir well to prevent clumping.
2. Cover and refrigerate overnight.
3. In the morning, top with berries and sliced almonds before serving.

BATCH-COOKING SUGGESTION: Make a few servings of chia pudding at once, storing them in the fridge for up to 4 days for a quick grab-and-go breakfast.

FETA & HERB COTTAGE CHEESE BOWL

PREP TIME: 5 MINUTES

DIETARY: Gluten-freeDairy-Free: Use dairy-free cottage cheese and omit feta.

250 CALORIES, 18G PROTEIN, 12G CARBS, 15G FAT

INGREDIENTS:

- ½ cup cottage cheese (or dairy-free alternative)
- 2 tbsp crumbled feta
- 1 tbsp fresh mint or parsley (chopped)
- 1 tsp olive oil
- Salt and pepper to taste

INSTRUCTIONS:

1. Mix cottage cheese, crumbled feta, and fresh herbs in a bowl.
2. Drizzle with olive oil and season with salt and pepper.
3. Serve immediately.

BATCH-COOKING SUGGESTION: Prep extra cottage cheese bowls and store in the fridge for quick breakfasts.

OATMEAL WITH PISTACHIOS, HONEY & DATES

PREP TIME: 10 MINUTES

DIETARY: Gluten-free, dairy-free, vegan

320 CALORIES, 8G PROTEIN, 50G CARBS, 12G FAT

INGREDIENTS:

- ½ cup oats
- 1 cup almond milk (or any plant-based milk)
- 1 tbsp honey (or maple syrup for vegan)
- 2 tbsp chopped dates
- 2 tbsp pistachios (chopped)

INSTRUCTIONS:

1. Bring almond milk to a boil in a small pot, then stir in oats and reduce heat.
2. Cook for 5 minutes, stirring occasionally, until thickened.
3. Remove from heat and stir in honey or maple syrup.
4. Top with chopped dates and pistachios before serving

BATCH-COOKING SUGGESTION: Cook a large batch of oatmeal, store in the fridge, and reheat throughout the week.

FALAFEL BREAKFAST BOWL

PREP TIME: 15 MINUTES

DIETARY : Naturally gluten-free, vegan

350 CALORIES, 12G PROTEIN, 40G CARBS, 15G FAT

INGREDIENTS:

- 4 pre-made falafel (store-bought or homemade)
- ½ cup quinoa
- ½ cucumber (chopped)
- ½ tomato (chopped)
- 2 tbsp hummus
- 1 tbsp olive oil

INSTRUCTIONS:

1. Cook quinoa according to package instructions.
2. Reheat falafel if necessary, then assemble the bowl by adding quinoa, chopped cucumber, tomato, and falafel.
3. Drizzle with olive oil and serve with hummus on the side

BATCH-COOKING SUGGESTION: Make a big batch of falafel and quinoa to use throughout the week in various meals.

15-MINUTE FEASTS

TILAPIA SAGANAKI

PREP TIME: 15 MINUTES
DIETARY: Gluten-free, dairy-free option

320 CALORIES, 25G PROTEIN, 10G CARBS, 16G FAT

INGREDIENTS:

- 2 tilapia fillets (cut into large chunks)
- 2 tbsp olive oil
- 2 cloves garlic (minced)
- 1 cup canned crushed tomatoes
- ¼ cup crumbled feta (optional)
- 1 tsp dried oregano
- Salt and pepper to taste
- Fresh parsley for garnish

INSTRUCTIONS:

1. Heat 1 tbsp olive oil in a skillet over medium heat. Add the minced garlic and cook for 1 minute until fragrant.
2. Add the crushed tomatoes, oregano, salt, and pepper. Simmer for 5 minutes to thicken the sauce slightly.
3. In a separate pan, heat the remaining olive oil and sear the tilapia chunks for 2-3 minutes on each side until cooked through and golden.
4. Gently stir the cooked tilapia into the tomato sauce.
5. If using, sprinkle with crumbled feta and garnish with fresh parsley before serving.

DAIRY-FREE: Omit the feta or use a dairy-free cheese alternative.

BATCH-COOKING SUGGESTION: Make extra tomato sauce and store it in the fridge for 2-3 days. It can be used with other proteins like chicken or as a pasta sauce.

LEFTOVER MAKEOVER: Leftover tilapia saganaki can be served over rice, quinoa, or pasta, or even as a filling for wraps.

SPICED CHICKEN SKEWERS WITH TZATZIKI

PREP TIME: 15 MINUTES
DIETARY: Gluten-free, dairy-free option

370 CALORIES, 28G PROTEIN, 10G CARBS, 20G FAT

INGREDIENTS:
- 2 boneless, skinless chicken breasts (cut into cubes)
- 1 tsp cumin
- 1 tsp coriander
- ½ tsp ground cinnamon
- 1 tbsp olive oil
- Salt and pepper to taste
- ¼ cup Greek yogurt (or dairy-free yogurt for tzatziki)
- ½ cucumber (grated)
- 1 tsp lemon juice
- Fresh parsley for garnish
- Wooden skewers (soaked in water if grilling)

INSTRUCTIONS:
1. In a bowl, toss the chicken cubes with cumin, coriander, cinnamon, olive oil, salt, and pepper.
2. Thread the chicken onto skewers and grill or pan-sear for 3-4 minutes on each side until fully cooked.
3. In a small bowl, mix the yogurt, grated cucumber, lemon juice, and a pinch of salt to make the tzatziki.
4. Serve the spiced chicken skewers with a dollop of tzatziki on the side and garnish with fresh parsley.

DAIRY-FREE: Use a dairy-free yogurt for the tzatziki or substitute with hummus.

BATCH-COOKING SUGGESTION: Make extra chicken skewers and store them in the fridge for up to 3 days. They're perfect for quick wraps, salads, or grain bowls.

LEFTOVER MAKEOVER: Leftover chicken can be sliced and added to salads or wraps, or used as a topping for couscous or quinoa.

GRILLED LEMON-HERB CHICKEN WITH OLIVE & CUCUMBER SALAD

PREP TIME: 15 MINUTES
DIETARY: Gluten-free, dairy-free, vegan option

400 CALORIES, 35G PROTEIN, 20G CARBS, 20G FAT

INGREDIENTS:
- 2 boneless, skinless chicken breasts
- 2 tbsp olive oil
- Juice of 1 lemon
- 1 tsp dried oregano
- ½ tsp garlic powder
- Salt and pepper to taste
- ½ cucumber (sliced)
- ¼ cup Kalamata olives (pitted and halved)
- 1 tbsp fresh parsley (chopped)

INSTRUCTIONS:
1. Heat a grill pan or skillet over medium-high heat.
2. In a small bowl, combine 1 tbsp olive oil, lemon juice, oregano, garlic powder, salt, and pepper. Rub this mixture over the chicken breasts.
3. Grill the chicken for 6-7 minutes on each side, until cooked through.
4. While the chicken cooks, toss the cucumber slices, olives, parsley, and remaining olive oil in a bowl. Season with salt and pepper.
5. Serve the grilled chicken alongside the cucumber and olive salad.

VEGAN: substitute the chicken with grilled tofu or portobello mushrooms.

BATCH-COOKING SUGGESTION: Grill extra chicken to use in

salads or wraps later in the week. The cucumber salad can be prepped and stored in the fridge for up to 2 days.

LEFTOVER MAKEOVER: Slice leftover chicken and add it to a grain bowl with couscous or quinoa, or use it in a pita wrap with hummus and veggies.

QUICK MEDITERRANEAN PASTA WITH OLIVES, CAPERS & CHERRY TOMATOES

PREP TIME: 15 MINUTES
DIETARY: Vegan, dairy-free, gluten-free option

50 CALORIES, 12G PROTEIN, 55G CARBS, 12G FAT

INGREDIENTS:

- 200g spaghetti (or gluten-free pasta)
- 1 tbsp olive oil
- 1 cup cherry tomatoes (halved)
- ¼ cup Kalamata olives (pitted and halved)
- 1 tbsp capers
- 1 clove garlic (minced)
- Fresh basil for garnish
- Salt and pepper to taste

INSTRUCTIONS:

1. Cook the pasta according to package instructions. Drain and set aside.
2. Heat olive oil in a skillet over medium heat. Add minced garlic and cook for 1 minute.
3. Stir in the cherry tomatoes, olives, and capers. Cook for 3-5 minutes, until the tomatoes soften slightly.
4. Toss the cooked pasta into the skillet and mix well. Season with salt and pepper.
5. Garnish with fresh basil and serve immediately.

GLUTEN-FREE: Use gluten-free pasta.

BATCH-COOKING SUGGESTION: Cook extra pasta and store it in the fridge for up to 3 days. Toss with olive oil to prevent sticking, and it's ready to go for quick lunches or dinners.

LEFTOVER MAKEOVER: Turn leftover pasta into a cold pasta salad by adding fresh veggies, herbs, and a drizzle of olive oil and lemon juice.

ONE-POT LEMON ORZO WITH SPINACH & CHICKPEAS

PREP TIME: 15 MINUTES
DIETARY: Vegan, dairy-free

340 CALORIES, 10G PROTEIN, 50G CARBS, 12G FAT

INGREDIENTS:

- 1 cup orzo (or gluten-free pasta)
- 2 cups vegetable broth
- 1 cup canned chickpeas (drained and rinsed)
- Juice and zest of 1 lemon
- 2 cups fresh spinach
- 1 tbsp olive oil
- Salt and pepper to taste

INSTRUCTIONS:

1. Heat olive oil in a large pan over medium heat. Add orzo and stir for 1-2 minutes until lightly toasted.
2. Add vegetable broth and bring to a simmer. Cook for 8-10 minutes until orzo is tender and most of the liquid is absorbed.
3. Stir in chickpeas, spinach, lemon juice, and zest. Cook for another 2-3 minutes until the spinach wilts.
4. Season with salt and pepper before serving.

GLUTEN-FREE: substitute the orzo with gluten-free pasta or quinoa.

BATCH-COOKING SUGGESTION: Make extra orzo and use it

for lunches throughout the week. It can be added to salads or served as a side for proteins.

LEFTOVER MAKEOVER: Use leftover lemon orzo as a base for a grain bowl or stir in additional veggies for a quick meal.

GARLIC AND HERB GRILLED HALLOUMI WITH COUSCOUS SALAD

PREP TIME: 15 MINUTES
DIETARY: Gluten-free option

370 CALORIES, 18G PROTEIN, 35G CARBS, 18G FAT

INGREDIENTS:

- 200g halloumi cheese (sliced)
- 1 cup couscous (or quinoa for gluten-free)
- 1 tbsp olive oil
- Juice of 1 lemon
- 1 cup cherry tomatoes (halved)
- 1 small cucumber (chopped)
- 1 tbsp fresh mint or parsley (chopped)
- Salt and pepper to taste

INSTRUCTIONS:

1. Prepare couscous according to package instructions (usually 5 minutes), then fluff with a fork and set aside.
2. Heat a grill pan over medium heat. Grill the halloumi slices for 2-3 minutes on each side until golden and crisp.
3. In a bowl, toss the couscous with olive oil, lemon juice, cherry tomatoes, cucumber, mint, salt, and pepper.
4. Serve the grilled halloumi over the couscous salad and garnish with extra mint.

GLUTEN-FREE: Use quinoa instead of couscous.

BATCH-COOKING SUGGESTION: Make extra couscous salad and store it for 2-3 days in the fridge. It's perfect for pairing with other proteins throughout the week.

LEFTOVER MAKEOVER: Leftover halloumi can be added to wraps, sandwiches, or reheated for a quick snack.

VEGETARIAN STUFFED PEPPERS WITH QUINOA & FETA

PREP TIME: 15 MINUTES
DIETARY: Gluten-free, dairy-free option, vegan option

360 CALORIES, 12G PROTEIN, 45G CARBS, 15G FAT

INGREDIENTS:

- 2 large bell peppers (halved and deseeded)
- 1 cup cooked quinoa (or couscous)
- 2 tbsp olive oil
- ¼ cup crumbled feta (optional)
- 1 cup spinach (chopped)
- 1 clove garlic (minced)
- Salt and pepper to taste
- Fresh parsley for garnish

INSTRUCTIONS:

1. Preheat the oven to 400°F (200°C).
2. Heat 1 tbsp olive oil in a skillet over medium heat Add garlic and spinach, cooking until wilted.
3. In a bowl, combine the cooked quinoa, spinach mixture, and crumbled feta. Season with salt and pepper.
4. Stuff the halved bell peppers with the quinoa mixture and place in a baking dish. Drizzle with remaining olive oil.
5. Bake for 10-12 minutes, until the peppers are tender. Garnish with parsley before serving.

DAIRY-FREE/VEGAN: Omit the feta or use a plant-based cheese alternative.

BATCH-COOKING SUGGESTION:
Make extra stuffed peppers and store them in the fridge for up to 3 days. They reheat well for a quick lunch or dinner.

LEFTOVER MAKEOVER: Leftover quinoa stuffing can be used in wraps or as a topping for salads.

PAN-SEARED SALMON WITH TOMATO & OLIVE RELISH

PREP TIME: 15 MINUTES
DIETARY: Gluten-free, dairy-free

420 CALORIES, 30G PROTEIN, 10G CARBS, 30G FAT

INGREDIENTS:

- 2 salmon fillets
- 1 tbsp olive oil
- 1 cup cherry tomatoes (halved)
- ¼ cup Kalamata olives (sliced)
- 1 tbsp capers
- Juice of 1 lemon
- Salt and pepper to taste
- Fresh parsley for garnish

INSTRUCTIONS:

1. Heat olive oil in a skillet over medium-high heat. Season the salmon fillets with salt and pepper.
2. Sear the salmon, skin-side down, for 4-5 minutes until the skin is crispy. Flip and cook for another 2-3 minutes until the salmon is cooked through.
3. While the salmon cooks, combine the cherry tomatoes, olives, capers, and lemon juice in a bowl.
4. Serve the salmon topped with the tomato and olive relish, and garnish with fresh parsley.

BATCH-COOKING SUGGESTION: Make extra tomato and olive relish to use as a topping for grilled chicken or as a dip for bread or crackers later.

LEFTOVER MAKEOVER: Leftover salmon can be flaked and used in salads, grain bowls, or even wraps for the next day.

SHAKSHUKA (EGGS IN SPICY TOMATO SAUCE)

PREP TIME: 15 MINUTES
DIETARY: Gluten-free, dairy-free

300 CALORIES, 15G PROTEIN, 20G CARBS, 18G FAT

INGREDIENTS:

- 4 eggs
- 1 can (14 oz) crushed tomatoes
- 1 bell pepper (chopped)
- 1 onion (chopped)
- 2 cloves garlic (minced)
- 1 tsp paprika
- 1 tsp cumin
- 1 tbsp olive oil
- Salt and pepper to taste
- Fresh parsley for garnish

INSTRUCTIONS:

1. Heat olive oil in a large skillet over medium heat. Add the chopped onion and bell pepper, cooking until softened (about 5 minutes).
2. Stir in the garlic, paprika, cumin, salt, and pepper. Cook for 1 minute.
3. Add the crushed tomatoes and simmer for 5 minutes.
4. Make small wells in the sauce and crack the eggs into each well. Cover and cook for 5-6 minutes, until the eggs are just set.

5. Garnish with fresh parsley and serve with crusty bread or pita.

BATCH-COOKING SUGGESTION: Make extra tomato sauce and store it in the fridge for up to 3 days. Reheat and add fresh eggs when ready to serve.

LEFTOVER MAKEOVER: Use leftover shakshuka sauce as a base for pasta, or spoon it over grilled vegetables for an easy dinner.

ZA'ATAR FLATBREAD PIZZAS

PREP TIME: 10 MINUTES
DIETARY: Gluten-free option, dairy-free option

330 CALORIES, 8G PROTEIN, 40G CARBS, 15G FAT

INGREDIENTS:

- 2 small flatbreads (or gluten-free wraps)
- 1 tbsp olive oil
- 2 tbsp za'atar spice blend
- 1 tomato (sliced)
- ¼ cup crumbled feta (or dairy-free cheese)
- Fresh parsley for garnish

INSTRUCTIONS:

1. Preheat the oven to 400°F (200°C).
2. Brush the flatbreads with olive oil and sprinkle with za'atar.
3. Top with tomato slices and crumbled feta.
4. Bake for 8-10 minutes, until the flatbreads are crisp and the cheese is slightly melted.
5. Garnish with fresh parsley and serve immediately.

GLUTEN-FREE: Use gluten-free flatbreads or wraps.
DAIRY-FREE: Use dairy-free cheese or omit the cheese altogether.

BATCH-COOKING SUGGESTION: Make extra flatbreads and store them in the fridge for up to 2 days. Reheat them in the oven for a quick snack or meal.

LEFTOVER MAKEOVER: Leftover flatbreads can be reheated for lunch or cut into smaller pieces and served as appetizers.

GARLIC SHRIMP WITH LEMON & PARSLEY

PREP TIME: 12 MINUTES
DIETARY: Gluten-free, dairy-free

290 CALORIES, 30G PROTEIN, 10G CARBS, 15G FAT

INGREDIENTS:

- 12 large shrimp (peeled and deveined)
- 2 tbsp olive oil
- 3 cloves garlic (minced)
- Juice of 1 lemon
- 1 tbsp fresh parsley (chopped)
- Salt and pepper to taste

INSTRUCTIONS:

6. Heat olive oil in a skillet over medium-high heat. Add the minced garlic and cook for 1 minute until fragrant.
7. Add the shrimp and cook for 2-3 minutes per side until pink and cooked through.
8. Remove from heat, drizzle with lemon juice, and sprinkle with fresh parsley.
9. Serve immediately with a side of grilled vegetables or over a salad.

BATCH-COOKING SUGGESTION: Make extra shrimp and use them cold in salads or wraps for the next couple of days.

LEFTOVER MAKEOVER: Leftover shrimp can be tossed with pasta, served in wraps, or added to grain bowls.

GRILLED CHICKEN SHAWARMA WITH TAHINI SAUCE

PREP TIME: 15 MINUTES
DIETARY: Gluten-free, dairy-free

400 CALORIES, 35G PROTEIN, 12G CARBS, 22G FAT

INGREDIENTS:

- 2 boneless, skinless chicken breasts (thinly sliced)
- 1 tbsp olive oil
- 1 tsp ground cumin
- 1 tsp ground coriander
- 1 tsp paprika
- ½ tsp turmeric
- Salt and pepper to taste
- ¼ cup tahini
- Juice of 1 lemon
- 2 tbsp water
- Fresh parsley for garnish

INSTRUCTIONS:

1. In a bowl, mix the olive oil, cumin, coriander, paprika, turmeric, salt, and pepper. Toss the sliced chicken in the spice mixture until fully coated.
2. Heat a grill pan or skillet over medium heat and cook the chicken for 3-4 minutes per side until cooked through.
3. In a small bowl, mix the tahini, lemon juice, water, and a pinch of salt until smooth.
4. Serve the grilled chicken with a drizzle of tahini sauce and garnish with fresh parsley.

BATCH-COOKING SUGGESTION: Grill extra chicken and store it in the fridge for up to 3 days. It's perfect for quick wraps or salads.

LEFTOVER MAKEOVER: Leftover chicken can be added to grain bowls, wraps, or served over a salad with the remaining tahini sauce.

MEDITERRANEAN STUFFED PITA WITH HUMMUS & GRILLED VEGGIES

PREP TIME: 15 MINUTES
DIETARY: Vegan, dairy-free, gluten-free option

340 CALORIES, 10G PROTEIN, 45G CARBS, 15G FAT

INGREDIENTS:

- 2 pita breads (or gluten-free pita)
- ½ cup hummus
- 1 zucchini (sliced)
- 1 red bell pepper (sliced)
- 1 tbsp olive oil
- 1 tsp za'atar
- Salt and pepper to taste

INSTRUCTIONS:

1. Heat olive oil in a skillet over medium heat. Add the zucchini and bell pepper, and cook for 5-7 minutes until tender.
2. Season the grilled vegetables with salt, pepper, and za'atar.
3. Cut the pita breads in half and spread hummus inside each pocket.
4. Stuff the pita with the grilled vegetables and serve.

GLUTEN-FREE: Use gluten-free pita or wraps.

BATCH-COOKING SUGGESTION: Grill extra veggies and store them in the fridge for up to 3 days. They can be added to sandwiches, wraps, or salads.

LEFTOVER MAKEOVER: Leftover grilled veggies can be used in grain bowls, pasta salads, or even tossed with couscous or quinoa for a quick meal.

MEDITERRANEAN TUNA SALAD WITH WHITE BEANS

PREP TIME: 10 MINUTES
DIETARY: Gluten-free, dairy-free

350 CALORIES, 25G PROTEIN, 20G CARBS, 18G FAT

INGREDIENTS:

- 1 can (5 oz) tuna (drained)
- 1 cup canned white beans (drained and rinsed)
- 1 small red onion (finely chopped)
- 1 tbsp olive oil
- Juice of 1 lemon
- 1 tbsp fresh parsley (chopped)
- Salt and pepper to taste

INSTRUCTIONS:

1. In a bowl, combine the tuna, white beans, red onion, olive oil, and lemon juice.
2. Season with salt and pepper and stir in the fresh parsley.
3. Serve immediately or refrigerate for later.

VEGAN: replace the tuna with canned chickpeas.

BATCH-COOKING SUGGESTION: Make a larger batch of the tuna salad and store in the fridge for up to 3 days. It's perfect for quick lunches or snacks.

LEFTOVER MAKEOVER: Use leftover tuna salad in wraps or as a topping for a Mediterranean-style grain bowl with quinoa or couscous.

CHICKPEA AND SPINACH STEW WITH HARISSA

PREP TIME: 15 MINUTES
DIETARY: Vegan, gluten-free, dairy-free

320 CALORIES, 12G PROTEIN, 50G CARBS, 10G FAT

INGREDIENTS:

- 1 can (15 oz) chickpeas (drained and rinsed)
- 2 cups fresh spinach
- 1 tbsp olive oil
- 1 onion (chopped)
- 2 garlic cloves (minced)
- 1 tsp cumin
- 1 tbsp harissa paste (or to taste)
- 1 can (14 oz) diced tomatoes
- Salt and pepper to taste

INSTRUCTIONS:

1. Heat olive oil in a skillet over medium heat. Add the onion and garlic, and cook for 3-4 minutes until softened.
2. Stir in the cumin and harissa paste, and cook for 1 minute.
3. Add the chickpeas and diced tomatoes. Simmer for 5 minutes.
4. Stir in the spinach and cook until wilted, about 2 minutes.
5. Season with salt and pepper and serve..

BATCH-COOKING SUGGESTION: Make a larger batch of the stew and store in the fridge for up to 3 days. It reheats well for quick lunches or dinners.

LEFTOVER MAKEOVER: Leftover chickpea stew can be served over rice, couscous, or quinoa, or used as a filling for wraps or pita sandwiches.

MEDITERRANEAN LENTIL SALAD WITH FETA & HERBS

PREP TIME: 15 MINUTES
DIETARY: Gluten-free, dairy-free option, vegan option

320 CALORIES, 18G PROTEIN, 40G CARBS, 12G FAT

INGREDIENTS:

- 1 cup cooked lentils (or canned lentils, drained)
- 1 tbsp olive oil
- Juice of 1 lemon
- 1 small cucumber (chopped)
- ¼ cup crumbled feta (optional)
- 1 tbsp fresh mint or parsley (chopped)
- Salt and pepper to taste

INSTRUCTIONS:

1. In a large bowl, combine the cooked lentils, chopped cucumber, olive oil, and lemon juice.
2. Stir in the crumbled feta (if using) and fresh herbs.
3. Season with salt and pepper, then serve.

DAIRY-FREE/VEGAN: Omit the feta or use a plant-based cheese alternative.

BATCH-COOKING SUGGESTION: Make extra lentil salad and store it in the fridge for 2-3 days

SPICED BEEF KOFTA WITH TAHINI DRIZZLE

PREP TIME: 15 MINUTES
DIETARY: Gluten-free, dairy-free

410 CALORIES, 25G PROTEIN, 10G CARBS, 30G FAT

INGREDIENTS:

- 200g ground beef (or lamb)
- 1 tsp cumin
- 1 tsp coriander
- ½ tsp cinnamon
- 1 clove garlic (minced)
- Salt and pepper to taste
- 2 tbsp tahini
- Juice of ½ lemon
- 2 tbsp water
- Fresh parsley for garnish

INSTRUCTIONS:

1. In a bowl, mix the ground beef with cumin, coriander, cinnamon, garlic, salt, and pepper. Shape the mixture into small patties or koftas.
2. Heat a grill pan or skillet over medium-high heat and cook the koftas for 4-5 minutes on each side until browned and cooked through.
3. In a small bowl, whisk together the tahini, lemon juice, water, and a pinch of salt to make the sauce.
4. Serve the koftas drizzled with tahini sauce and garnished with fresh parsley.

BATCH-COOKING SUGGESTION: Make extra koftas and store them in the fridge for 2-3 days. They reheat well for a quick lunch or dinner.

LEFTOVER MAKEOVER: Leftover koftas can be used in wraps, served over couscous, or added to grain bowls.

GREEK-STYLE TURKEY BURGERS WITH TZATZIKI

PREP TIME: 15 MINUTES
DIETARY: Gluten-free option, dairy-free option

350 CALORIES, 28G PROTEIN, 10G CARBS, 18G FAT

INGREDIENTS:

- 200g ground turkey
- 1 tsp dried oregano
- 1 clove garlic (minced)
- 1 tbsp olive oil
- ¼ cup Greek yogurt (or dairy-free yogurt for tzatziki)
- ½ cucumber (grated)
- 1 tsp lemon juice
- Salt and pepper to taste

INSTRUCTIONS:

1. In a bowl, combine the ground turkey, oregano, garlic, salt, and pepper. Shape into patties.
2. Heat olive oil in a skillet over medium heat and cook the turkey patties for 5-6 minutes on each side until cooked through.
3. In a small bowl, mix the yogurt, grated cucumber, lemon juice, and a pinch of salt to make tzatziki.
4. Serve the turkey burgers with a dollop of tzatziki

and your favorite side.

GLUTEN-FREE: Serve the burgers on gluten-free buns or lettuce wraps.

DAIRY-FREE: Use a dairy-free yogurt for the tzatziki.

BATCH-COOKING SUGGESTION: Double the turkey mixture and cook extra patties. They store well in the fridge for up to 3 days.

LEFTOVER MAKEOVER: Leftover turkey patties can be sliced and used in salads, grain bowls, or wraps.

BAKED COD WITH TOMATO-CAPER SALSA

PREP TIME: 15 MINUTES
DIETARY: Gluten-free, dairy-free

320 CALORIES, 30G PROTEIN, 10G CARBS, 15G FAT

INGREDIENTS:

- 2 cod fillets
- 1 tbsp olive oil
- Salt and pepper to taste
- Tomato-Caper Salsa:
- 1 cup cherry tomatoes (quartered)
- 2 tbsp capers (rinsed)
- ¼ cup Kalamata olives (chopped)
- 1 clove garlic (minced)
- 1 tbsp olive oil

- Juice of 1 lemon
- Fresh parsley for garnish
- Salt and pepper to taste

INSTRUCTIONS:

1. Preheat the oven to 400°F (200°C). Line a baking sheet with parchment paper.
2. Rub the cod fillets with olive oil, and season with salt and pepper.
3. Place the fillets on the baking sheet and bake for 12-15 minutes, or until the cod flakes easily with a fork.
4. While the cod is baking, combine the cherry tomatoes, capers, olives, garlic, olive oil, lemon juice, salt, and pepper in a bowl. Stir to mix well.
5. Once the cod is done baking, top each fillet with the tomato-caper salsa. Garnish with fresh parsley and serve immediately.

BATCH-COOKING SUGGESTION: Make extra salsa and store it in the fridge for up to 2 days. It can be used as a topping for other proteins like chicken or as a side dish.

LEFTOVER MAKEOVER: Leftover baked cod can be flaked and added to salads, grain bowls, or even tacos.

SAUTÉED MUSHROOMS & ZUCCHINI WITH GARLIC AND HERBS

PREP TIME: 10 MINUTES
DIETARY: Vegan, gluten-free, dairy-free

220 CALORIES, 6G PROTEIN, 10G CARBS, 16G FAT

INGREDIENTS:

- 1 cup mushrooms (sliced)
- 1 zucchini (sliced)
- 2 tbsp olive oil
- 2 cloves garlic (minced)
- 1 tsp dried thyme
- Salt and pepper to taste
- Fresh parsley for garnish

INSTRUCTIONS:

1. Heat olive oil in a skillet over medium heat. Add the garlic and cook for 1 minute.

2. Add the mushrooms and zucchini to the skillet, and sauté for 5-7 minutes until tender and golden.
3. Season with thyme, salt, and pepper.
4. Garnish with fresh parsley and serve.

BATCH-COOKING SUGGESTION: Make extra sautéed vegetables and store them in the fridge for up to 3 days. They can be reheated and used in various dishes.

LEFTOVER MAKEOVER: Leftover sautéed veggies can be added to pasta, used as a topping for toast, or served in wraps or bowls.

CHICKEN STIR-FRY WITH PEPPERS & OLIVES

PREP TIME: 15 MINUTES
DIETARY: Gluten-free, dairy-free

80 CALORIES, 30G PROTEIN, 20G CARBS, 18G FAT

INGREDIENTS:

- 2 boneless, skinless chicken breasts (sliced)
- 1 red bell pepper (sliced)
- 1 yellow bell pepper (sliced)
- ¼ cup Kalamata olives (sliced)
- 1 tbsp olive oil
- 1 tsp dried oregano
- Salt and pepper to taste

INSTRUCTIONS:

1. Heat olive oil in a skillet over medium heat. Add the sliced chicken and cook for 5-6 minutes, stirring occasionally.
2. Add the bell peppers and cook for another 4-5 minutes until the peppers are tender and the chicken is fully cooked.
3. Stir in the Kalamata olives, oregano, salt, and pepper. Cook for an additional 1-2 minutes.
4. Serve with a side of couscous, quinoa, or over greens.

BATCH-COOKING SUGGESTION: Cook extra chicken and veggies and store them in the fridge for up to 3 days. They can be used for quick lunches or dinners later.

LEFTOVER MAKEOVER: Leftover chicken stir-fry can be added to grain bowls, served in wraps, or tossed with pasta for a quick meal.

QUICK MOROCCAN-SPICED BEEF SKEWERS

PREP TIME: 15 MINUTES
DIETARY: Gluten-free, dairy-free

430 CALORIES, 28G PROTEIN, 10G CARBS, 30G FAT

INGREDIENTS:

- 200g ground beef
- 1 tsp ground cumin
- 1 tsp ground coriander
- ½ tsp cinnamon
- 1 tbsp olive oil
- Salt and pepper to taste
- Fresh mint for garnish

INSTRUCTIONS:

1. In a bowl, mix the ground beef with cumin, coriander, cinnamon, salt, and pepper.
2. Form the beef into small patties or onto skewers.
3. Heat olive oil in a grill pan over medium-high heat. Cook the skewers for 4-5 minutes on each side until fully cooked.
4. Garnish with fresh mint and serve with a side of couscous or grilled vegetables.

BATCH-COOKING SUGGESTION: Double the beef mixture and cook extra skewers. They can be stored in the fridge for up to 3 days and reheated for quick meals.

LEFTOVER MAKEOVER: Leftover beef skewers can be used in wraps or sliced and added to salads or grain bowls.

LEMON GARLIC GRILLED SHRIMP WITH COUSCOUS

PREP TIME: 15 MINUTES
DIETARY: Gluten-free option, dairy-free

350 CALORIES, 30G PROTEIN, 40G CARBS, 12G FAT

INGREDIENTS:

- 12 large shrimp (peeled and deveined)
- 1 cup couscous (or quinoa for gluten-free)
- 1 tbsp olive oil
- Juice of 1 lemon

- 2 cloves garlic (minced)
- Salt and pepper to taste
- Fresh parsley for garnish

INSTRUCTIONS:

1. Cook the couscous according to package instructions (usually 5 minutes), then fluff with a fork and set aside.
2. In a bowl, toss the shrimp with olive oil, minced garlic, lemon juice, salt, and pepper.
3. Heat a grill pan over medium heat. Grill the shrimp for 2-3 minutes on each side until pink and fully cooked.
4. Serve the shrimp over the couscous and garnish with fresh parsley.

GLUTEN-FREE: Use quinoa instead of couscous.

BATCH-COOKING SUGGESTION: Make extra couscous to use in salads or as a base for other meals during the week.

LEFTOVER MAKEOVER: Leftover shrimp and couscous can be tossed with fresh veggies for a light shrimp salad or added to a grain bowl.

MEDITERRANEAN CHICKEN WRAP WITH HUMMUS & VEGGIES

PREP TIME: 15 MINUTES
DIETARY: Gluten-free option, dairy-free

380 CALORIES, 32G PROTEIN, 30G CARBS, 14G FAT

INGREDIENTS:

- 2 boneless, skinless chicken breasts (grilled or cooked and sliced)
- 2 whole wheat wraps (or gluten-free wraps)
- 4 tbsp hummus
- ½ cucumber (sliced)
- 1 tomato (sliced)
- 1 small red onion (thinly sliced)
- 1 tbsp olive oil
- Salt and pepper to taste

INSTRUCTIONS:

1. Heat the wraps in a pan or microwave for a few seconds to soften.
2. Spread 2 tbsp hummus on each wrap.

3. Layer the grilled chicken, cucumber, tomato, and red onion on top.
4. Drizzle with olive oil, season with salt and pepper and roll up the wraps.
5. Serve immediately.

GLUTEN-FREE: Use gluten-free wraps.

BATCH-COOKING SUGGESTION: Grill extra chicken and store it for up to 3 days. This makes assembling wraps quick and easy for the rest of the week.

LEFTOVER MAKEOVER: Use leftover chicken and veggies in salads, grain bowls, or pita sandwiches.

GRILLED PORK CHOPS WITH MINT PESTO

PREP TIME: 15 MINUTES
DIETARY: Gluten-free, dairy-free

430 CALORIES, 32G PROTEIN, 12G CARBS, 26G FAT

INGREDIENTS:

- 2 boneless pork chops
- 1 tbsp olive oil
- Salt and pepper to taste
- Mint Pesto:
- 1 cup fresh mint leaves
- ¼ cup almonds or pine nuts
- 1 clove garlic

- Juice of 1 lemon
- ¼ cup olive oil
- Salt and pepper to taste

INSTRUCTIONS:

1. Heat a grill pan or outdoor grill over medium-high heat. Brush the pork chops with olive oil and season generously with salt and pepper.
2. Grill for about 4-5 minutes on each side, until cooked through (internal temperature should reach 145°F or 63°C).
3. While the pork chops are grilling, combine the mint leaves, almonds, garlic, lemon juice, and olive oil in a food processor. Blend until smooth. Season with salt and pepper to taste.
4. Once the pork chops are done, top with a generous spoonful of mint pesto. Serve immediately.

BATCH-COOKING SUGGESTION: Make extra mint pesto and store it in the fridge for up to a week. It's great for drizzling over grilled veggies, chicken, or pasta.

LEFTOVER MAKEOVER: Leftover pork can be sliced and added to sandwiches, wraps, or grain bowls.

QUICK MEDITERRANEAN MEATBALLS WITH TZATZIKI

PREP TIME: 15 MINUTES
DIETARY: Gluten-free, dairy-free option

360 CALORIES, 25G PROTEIN, 15G CARBS, 22G FAT

INGREDIENTS:

- 200g ground beef (or lamb)
- 1 tsp cumin
- 1 tsp paprika
- 1 clove garlic (minced)
- 1 tbsp olive oil
- ¼ cup Greek yogurt (or dairy-free yogurt for tzatziki)
- ½ cucumber (grated)
- Juice of ½ lemon
- Salt and pepper to taste

INSTRUCTIONS:

1. In a bowl, mix the ground beef, cumin, paprika, garlic, salt, and pepper. Form into small meatballs.
2. Heat olive oil in a skillet over medium heat and cook the meatballs for 4-5 minutes on each side until browned and fully cooked.
3. In a small bowl, mix the yogurt, grated cucumber, lemon juice, and a pinch of salt to make tzatziki.
4. Serve the meatballs with tzatziki on the side.

DAIRY-FREE: Use dairy-free yogurt for the tzatziki.

BATCH-COOKING SUGGESTION: Double the meatball mixture and cook extra. Store them in the fridge for up to 3 days for quick lunches or dinners.

LEFTOVER MAKEOVER: Leftover meatballs can be used in wraps, added to salads, or served over grains.

EGGPLANT & ZUCCHINI STIR-FRY WITH GARLIC AND PINE NUTS

PREP TIME: 15 MINUTES
DIETARY: Vegan, gluten-free, dairy-free

280 CALORIES, 6G PROTEIN, 20G CARBS, 20G FAT

INGREDIENTS:

- 1 small eggplant (cubed)
- 1 zucchini (sliced)
- 2 tbsp olive oil
- 2 cloves garlic (minced)
- 2 tbsp pine nuts (toasted)
- Salt and pepper to taste
- Fresh parsley for garnish

INSTRUCTIONS:

1. Heat 1 tbsp olive oil in a skillet over medium heat. Add the eggplant cubes and cook for 5-7 minutes until tender and slightly golden.
2. Add the zucchini slices, garlic, and remaining olive oil to the skillet. Cook for another 3-4 minutes until the zucchini is tender.
3. Season with salt and pepper, then sprinkle with toasted pine nuts and fresh parsley. Serve immediately.

BATCH-COOKING SUGGESTION: Make extra stir-fry and store it in the fridge for up to 2 days. Reheat for a quick lunch or dinner.

LEFTOVER MAKEOVER: Leftover stir-fry can be added to pasta or grain bowls or used as a topping for toast or pizza.

SAUTÉED CALAMARI WITH LEMON & GARLIC

PREP TIME: 12 MINUTES
DIETARY: Gluten-free, dairy-free

240 CALORIES, 20G PROTEIN, 8G CARBS, 14G FAT

INGREDIENTS:

- 200g calamari (cleaned and sliced into rings)
- 2 tbsp olive oil
- 2 cloves garlic (minced)
- Juice of 1 lemon
- Salt and pepper to taste
- Fresh parsley for garnish

INSTRUCTIONS:

4. Heat olive oil in a skillet over medium-high heat. Add the garlic and cook for 1 minute until fragrant.
5. Add the calamari rings and sauté for 2-3 minutes, stirring occasionally, until the calamari turns opaque and tender.
6. Remove from heat, drizzle with lemon juice, and season with salt and pepper.
7. Garnish with fresh parsley and serve.

BATCH-COOKING SUGGESTION: Calamari is best eaten fresh, but the lemon-garlic sauce can be made in advance and stored for up to 3 days.

LEFTOVER MAKEOVER: Leftover calamari can be tossed into salads, served over pasta, or used in wraps.

GRILLED MAHI-MAHI WITH OLIVE TAPENADE

PREP TIME: 15 MINUTES
DIETARY: Gluten-free, dairy-free

380 CALORIES, 35G PROTEIN, 10G CARBS, 22G FAT

INGREDIENTS:

- 2 mahi-mahi fillets
- 1 tbsp olive oil
- Salt and pepper to taste

Olive Tapenade:

- ½ cup Kalamata olives (pitted and chopped)
- 1 tbsp capers (rinsed)
- 1 clove garlic (minced)
- 1 tbsp fresh parsley (chopped)
- Juice of 1 lemon
- 1 tbsp olive oil
- Salt and pepper to taste

INSTRUCTIONS:

1. Heat a grill pan or outdoor grill over medium-high heat.

2. Rub the mahi-mahi fillets with olive oil and season with salt and pepper.

3. Grill for 3-4 minutes on each side, or until the fish is cooked through and has grill marks.

4. In a small bowl, mix the chopped olives, capers, garlic, parsley, lemon juice, olive oil, salt, and pepper. Stir to combine.

5. Once the mahi-mahi is grilled, top each fillet with a generous spoonful of the olive tapenade. Serve immediately, garnished with extra parsley if desired.

BATCH-COOKING SUGGESTION: Make extra olive tapenade and store it in the fridge for up to 3 days. It's great as a topping for chicken, sandwiches, or even as a dip.

LEFTOVER MAKEOVER: Leftover mahi-mahi can be flaked and used in salads, tacos, or grain bowls.

PAN-SEARED CHICKEN THIGHS WITH OLIVES & SUNDRIED TOMATOES

PREP TIME: 15 MINUTES
DIETARY: Gluten-free, dairy-free

00 CALORIES, 30G PROTEIN, 12G CARBS, 24G FAT

INGREDIENTS:

4 boneless, skinless chicken thighs
1 tbsp olive oil
¼ cup Kalamata olives (halved)
¼ cup sundried tomatoes (chopped)
2 cloves garlic (minced)
Salt and pepper to taste
Fresh basil for garnish

INSTRUCTIONS:

1. Heat olive oil in a skillet over medium heat. Season the chicken thighs with salt and pepper.

2. Cook the chicken thighs for 5-6 minutes on each side until browned and cooked through.

3. Add the olives, sundried tomatoes, and garlic to the pan and cook for another 2-3 minutes, stirring occasionally.

4. Garnish with fresh basil and serve immediately.

BATCH-COOKING SUGGESTION: Make extra chicken thighs and store them in the fridge for up to 3 days. They're perfect for quick lunches or dinners.

LEFTOVER MAKEOVER: Leftover chicken can be shredded and used in wraps, salads, or grain bowls.

SPICED LENTIL PATTIES WITH HARISSA YOGURT

PREP TIME: 15 MINUTES
DIETARY: Gluten-free, dairy-free option, vegan option

320 CALORIES, 18G PROTEIN, 40G CARBS, 12G FAT

INGREDIENTS:

- 1 cup cooked lentils (or canned lentils, drained)
- 1 tbsp olive oil
- 1 clove garlic (minced)
- 1 tsp cumin
- 1 tsp paprika
- ¼ cup breadcrumbs (or gluten-free breadcrumbs)
- ¼ cup Greek yogurt (or dairy-free yogurt)
- 1 tsp harissa paste
- Salt and pepper to taste

INSTRUCTIONS:

1. In a bowl, mash the cooked lentils with olive oil, garlic, cumin, paprika, and breadcrumbs. Form into small patties.

2. Heat a skillet over medium heat and cook the pat-

ties for 3-4 minutes on each side until golden.
3. In a small bowl, mix the yogurt and harissa paste.
4. Serve the lentil patties with a dollop of harissa yogurt.

GLUTEN-FREE: Use gluten-free breadcrumbs.
DAIRY-FREE/VEGAN: Use dairy-free yogurt for the harissa sauce or substitute the yogurt with tahini.

BATCH-COOKING SUGGESTION: Make extra lentil patties and store them in the fridge for up to 3 days. They can be reheated for quick lunches or dinners.

LEFTOVER MAKEOVER: Leftover lentil patties can be used in wraps, grain bowls, or served with a side salad.

QUICK CHICKEN SKEWERS WITH GARLIC YOGURT SAUCE

PREP TIME: 15 MINUTES
DIETARY: Gluten-free, dairy-free option

390 CALORIES, 30G PROTEIN, 12G CARBS, 22G FAT

INGREDIENTS:
- 2 boneless, skinless chicken breasts (cut into cubes)
- 1 tbsp olive oil
- 1 tsp paprika
- 1 tsp dried oregano
- 1 clove garlic (minced)
- ¼ cup Greek yogurt (or dairy-free yogurt)
- Juice of 1 lemon
- Salt and pepper to taste
- Wooden skewers (soaked in water if grilling)

INSTRUCTIONS:
1. In a bowl, toss the chicken cubes with olive oil, paprika, oregano, garlic, salt, and pepper.
2. Thread the chicken onto skewers and grill or pan-sear for 3-4 minutes on each side until cooked through.
3. In a small bowl, mix the yogurt, lemon juice, and a pinch of salt to make the garlic yogurt sauce.
4. Serve the chicken skewers with the garlic yogurt sauce on the side.

DAIRY-FREE: Use dairy-free yogurt or serve with hummus instead of yogurt.

BATCH-COOKING SUGGESTION: Make extra chicken skewers and store them in the fridge for up to 3 days for easy meals throughout the week.

LEFTOVER MAKEOVER: Leftover chicken skewers can be used in wraps, salads, or served with a grain bowl.

SPAGHETTI AGLIO E OLIO WITH SPINACH

PREP TIME: 15 MINUTES
DIETARY: Vegan, gluten-free option, dairy-free

380 CALORIES, 10G PROTEIN, 55G CARBS, 12G FAT

INGREDIENTS:
- 200g spaghetti (or gluten-free pasta)
- 2 tbsp olive oil
- 3 cloves garlic (thinly sliced)
- 2 cups fresh spinach
- 1 tsp red pepper flakes
- Salt and pepper to taste
- Fresh parsley for garnish

INSTRUCTIONS:
1. Cook the spaghetti according to package instructions. Drain and set aside.
2. Heat olive oil in a skillet over medium heat. Add the garlic and red pepper flakes, and cook for 1-2 minutes until fragrant.
3. Add the spinach to the skillet and cook until wilted, about 2-3 minutes.
4. Toss the cooked spaghetti in the garlic and spinach mixture. Season with salt and pepper.
5. Garnish with fresh parsley and serve.

GLUTEN-FREE: Use gluten-free pasta.

BATCH-COOKING SUGGESTION: Make extra pasta and store it in the fridge for up to 3 days. It can be reheated or served cold as a pasta salad.

LEFTOVER MAKEOVER: Leftover spaghetti can be tossed with fresh veggies or served with grilled chicken or shrimp for a more substantial meal.

GRILLED CHICKEN PAILLARD WITH ARUGULA & PARMESAN

PREP TIME: 15 MINUTES
DIETARY: Gluten-free, dairy-free option

370 CALORIES, 35G PROTEIN, 10G CARBS, 18G FAT

INGREDIENTS:

- 2 boneless, skinless chicken breasts (pounded thin)
- 1 tbsp olive oil
- Juice of 1 lemon
- 2 cups arugula
- ¼ cup shaved Parmesan (optional)
- Salt and pepper to taste

INSTRUCTIONS:

1. Heat a grill pan over medium heat. Season the chicken breasts with salt, pepper, and olive oil.
2. Grill the chicken for 3-4 minutes per side until cooked through.
3. In a bowl, toss the arugula with lemon juice, olive oil, salt, and pepper.
4. Serve the grilled chicken topped with the arugula salad and shaved Parmesan (if using).

DAIRY-FREE: Omit the Parmesan or use a dairy-free cheese alternative.

BATCH-COOKING SUGGESTION: Grill extra chicken and store it in the fridge for up to 3 days. Use it for quick meals throughout the week.

LEFTOVER MAKEOVER: Leftover chicken can be sliced and used in sandwiches, wraps, or served over quinoa or couscous.

GRILLED HARISSA CHICKEN THIGHS WITH HERB YOGURT

PREP TIME: 15 MINUTES
DIETARY: Gluten-free, dairy-free option

400 CALORIES, 35G PROTEIN, 10G CARBS, 22G FAT

INGREDIENTS:

- 4 boneless, skinless chicken thighs
- 2 tbsp harissa paste
- 1 tbsp olive oil
- ¼ cup Greek yogurt (or dairy-free yogurt)
- 1 tbsp fresh mint (chopped)
- Juice of ½ lemon
- Salt and pepper to taste

INSTRUCTIONS:

1. Toss the chicken thighs with harissa paste, olive oil, salt, and pepper.
2. Heat a grill pan over medium-high heat and grill the chicken for 5-6 minutes on each side until fully cooked.
3. In a small bowl, mix the yogurt, mint, lemon juice, and a pinch of salt to make the herb yogurt sauce.
4. Serve the grilled harissa chicken with the herb yogurt on the side.

GLUTEN-FREE: This recipe is naturally gluten-free.
DAIRY-FREE: Use a dairy-free yogurt for the herb sauce.

BATCH-COOKING SUGGESTION: Make extra chicken thighs and store them in the fridge for up to 3 days. They're great for wraps, salads, or grain bowls.

LEFTOVER MAKEOVER: Leftover harissa chicken can be sliced and used in sandwiches, wraps, or added to couscous or quinoa bowls.

MOROCCAN CHICKEN TAGINE WITH APRICOTS & ALMONDS

PREP TIME: 15 MINUTES
DIETARY: Gluten-free, dairy-free

400 CALORIES, 30G PROTEIN, 20G CARBS, 20G FAT

INGREDIENTS:

- 2 boneless, skinless chicken thighs
- 1 tbsp olive oil
- 1 tsp ground cinnamon
- 1 tsp ground cumin
- 1 clove garlic (minced)
- ¼ cup dried apricots (chopped)
- 2 tbsp sliced almonds (toasted)
- Salt and pepper to taste

INSTRUCTIONS:

1. Heat olive oil in a skillet over medium heat. Season the chicken thighs with salt, pepper, cinnamon, and cumin.
2. Cook the chicken for 5-6 minutes on each side until browned and fully cooked.
3. Stir in the chopped apricots and garlic, and cook for another 2-3 minutes.
4. Garnish with toasted almonds and serve.

BATCH-COOKING SUGGESTION: Make extra chicken tagine and store it in the fridge for up to 3 days. It reheats well for quick lunches or dinners.

LEFTOVER MAKEOVER: Leftover chicken tagine can be served over couscous, quinoa, or rice for a heartier meal.

SARDINE TACOS WITH GARLIC-LEMON DRESSING

PREP TIME: 12 MINUTES
DIETARY: Gluten-free, dairy-free

320 CALORIES, 20G PROTEIN, 25G CARBS, 18G FAT

INGREDIENTS:

- 2 cans of sardines (in olive oil, drained)
- 4 corn tortillas (or gluten-free tortillas)
- 1 small cucumber (thinly sliced)
- 1 small red onion (thinly sliced)
- 1 tbsp olive oil
- Juice of 1 lemon
- 1 clove garlic (minced)
- Fresh parsley for garnish
- Salt and pepper to taste

INSTRUCTIONS:

1. Warm the corn tortillas in a dry skillet or microwave.
2. In a small bowl, mix the olive oil, lemon juice, gar-lic, salt, and pepper to make the dressing.
3. Divide the sardines among the tortillas, then top with cucumber slices and red onion.
4. Drizzle the garlic-lemon dressing over the tacos and garnish with fresh parsley. Serve immediately.

BATCH-COOKING SUGGESTION: The garlic-lemon dressing can be made ahead and stored in the fridge for up to a week.

LEFTOVER MAKEOVER: Leftover sardines can be mashed and mixed with herbs for a quick spread to enjoy with crackers or toast the next day.

GRILLED TURKEY KEBABS WITH CUCUMBER MINT SALAD

PREP TIME: 15 MINUTES
DIETARY: Gluten-free, dairy-free

380 CALORIES, 30G PROTEIN, 12G CARBS, 22G FAT

INGREDIENTS:

- 200g ground turkey
- 1 tsp ground cumin
- 1 tsp paprika
- 1 clove garlic (minced)
- 1 tbsp olive oil
- Salt and pepper to taste
- ½ cucumber (sliced)

- 1 tbsp fresh mint (chopped)
- Juice of 1 lemon
- Wooden skewers (soaked in water if grilling)

INSTRUCTIONS:

1. In a bowl, mix the ground turkey with cumin, paprika, garlic, salt, and pepper. Form the mixture into small kebabs and thread them onto skewers.
2. Heat a grill pan or skillet over medium-high heat and cook the turkey kebabs for 4-5 minutes on each side until fully cooked.
3. In a separate bowl, mix the cucumber slices, mint, lemon juice, olive oil, salt, and pepper to make the cucumber mint salad.
4. Serve the grilled turkey kebabs with the cucumber mint salad on the side.

BATCH-COOKING SUGGESTION: Make extra turkey kebabs and store them in the fridge for up to 3 days. They're great for wraps, salads, or quick meals.

LEFTOVER MAKEOVER: Leftover turkey kebabs can be sliced and added to salads, used in wraps, or served with couscous or rice for a quick meal.

QUICK LAMB AND FETA WRAPS WITH TZATZIKI

PREP TIME: 15 MINUTES
DIETARY: Gluten-free option, dairy-free option

420 CALORIES, 30G PROTEIN, 30G CARBS, 18G FAT

INGREDIENTS:

- 200g ground lamb
- 1 tsp cumin
- 1 tsp dried oregano
- 1 tbsp olive oil
- ¼ cup crumbled feta (optional)
- 4 tbsp tzatziki (or dairy-free yogurt sauce)
- 2 whole wheat wraps (or gluten-free wraps)
- Salt and pepper to taste

INSTRUCTIONS:

1. Heat olive oil in a skillet over medium heat. Add the ground lamb, cumin, oregano, salt, and pepper. Cook for 5-7 minutes, stirring occasionally, until browned and fully cooked.
2. Warm the wraps in a dry skillet or microwave.
3. Spread tzatziki on each wrap, then top with the cooked lamb and crumbled feta (if using).
4. Roll up the wraps and serve immediately.

GLUTEN-FREE: Use gluten-free wraps.
DAIRY-FREE: Omit the feta and use a dairy-free tzatziki alternative.

BATCH-COOKING SUGGESTION: Make extra lamb and store it in the fridge for up to 3 days. It can be used in various dishes like salads, grain bowls, or more wraps.

LEFTOVER MAKEOVER:
Leftover lamb can be used in stuffed peppers, added to pasta, or mixed with quinoa for a quick meal.

SEARED TUNA STEAKS WITH OLIVE & CAPER RELISH

PREP TIME: 15 MINUTES
DIETARY: Gluten-free, dairy-free

420 CALORIES, 35G PROTEIN, 8G CARBS, 25G FAT

INGREDIENTS:

- 2 tuna steaks
- 1 tbsp olive oil
- ¼ cup Kalamata olives (chopped)
- 1 tbsp capers (rinsed)

- Juice of 1 lemon
- 1 clove garlic (minced)
- Salt and pepper to taste
- Fresh parsley for garnish

INSTRUCTIONS:

1. Heat olive oil in a skillet over medium-high heat. Season the tuna steaks with salt and pepper.
2. Sear the tuna for 2-3 minutes on each side for medium-rare, or longer if desired.
3. In a small bowl, mix the chopped olives, capers, lemon juice, garlic, and a pinch of salt to make the relish.
4. Serve the tuna steaks topped with the olive and caper relish, garnished with fresh parsley.

BATCH-COOKING SUGGESTION: The olive-caper relish can be made in advance and stored in the fridge for up to 3 days.

LEFTOVER MAKEOVER: Leftover tuna can be flaked and used in salads or grain bowls.

MEDITERRANEAN VEGGIE FRITTATA

PREP TIME: 15 MINUTES
DIETARY: Gluten-free, dairy-free option, vegetarian

320 CALORIES, 18G PROTEIN, 8G CARBS, 22G FAT

INGREDIENTS:

- 4 large eggs
- 1 small zucchini (sliced)
- ½ cup cherry tomatoes (halved)
- 1 tbsp olive oil
- ¼ cup crumbled feta (optional)
- Salt and pepper to taste
- Fresh basil for garnish

INSTRUCTIONS:

1. Preheat the oven to 375°F (190°C).
2. Heat olive oil in a small oven-safe skillet over medium heat. Add the zucchini and cherry tomatoes, and cook for 4-5 minutes until softened.
3. In a bowl, whisk the eggs with salt and pepper, then pour over the vegetables in the skillet.
4. Sprinkle with crumbled feta (if using) and cook for 2-3 minutes on the stovetop.

5. Transfer the skillet to the oven and bake for 5-6 minutes until the frittata is set.
6. Garnish with fresh basil and serve.

DAIRY-FREE: Omit the feta or use a dairy-free cheese alternative.

BATCH-COOKING SUGGESTION: Make extra frittata and store it in the fridge for up to 2 days. It can be enjoyed cold or reheated for a quick breakfast or lunch.

LEFTOVER MAKEOVER: Leftover frittata can be used in sandwiches or wraps, or served with a side salad for a light meal.

FALAFEL-STUFFED PITA WITH TAHINI DRESSING

PREP TIME: 15 MINUTES
DIETARY: Vegan, gluten-free option

340 CALORIES, 10G PROTEIN, 40G CARBS, 15G FAT

INGREDIENTS:

- 6 falafel (store-bought or homemade)
- 2 pita breads (or gluten-free pita)
- ½ cucumber (sliced)
- 1 small tomato (sliced)
- 2 tbsp tahini
- Juice of 1 lemon
- 2 tbsp water
- Salt and pepper to taste

INSTRUCTIONS:

1. Warm the pita breads in a dry skillet or microwave.
2. In a small bowl, mix the tahini, lemon juice, water, salt, and pepper to make the dressing.
3. Stuff each pita with falafel, cucumber slices, and tomato slices.
4. Drizzle with tahini dressing and serve.

GLUTEN-FREE: Use gluten-free pita.

BATCH-COOKING SUGGESTION: Make extra tahini dressing and store it in the fridge for up to 1 week. It can be used in wraps, salads, or as a dip for veggies.

LEFTOVER MAKEOVER: Leftover falafel can be served over a salad or grain bowl, or added to wraps.

PAN-FRIED HALLOUMI WITH LEMON & ZA'ATAR

PREP TIME: 12 MINUTES
DIETARY: Gluten-free, vegetarian

380 CALORIES, 20G PROTEIN, 8G CARBS, 28G FAT

INGREDIENTS:

- 200g halloumi cheese (sliced)
- 1 tbsp olive oil
- Juice of ½ lemon
- 1 tsp za'atar
- Fresh mint for garnish

INSTRUCTIONS:

1. Heat olive oil in a skillet over medium heat. Add the halloumi slices and cook for 2-3 minutes on each side until golden brown and crispy.
2. Remove from the skillet and drizzle with lemon juice and sprinkle with za'atar.
3. Garnish with fresh mint and serve immediately.

BATCH-COOKING SUGGESTION: Halloumi is best served fresh, but the lemon-za'atar topping can be made in advance and stored in the fridge for up to 3 days.

LEFTOVER MAKEOVER: Leftover halloumi can be added to salads, wraps, or served with grilled vegetables.

SIDES

MEDITERRANEAN SPICED RICE

PREP TIME: 15 MINUTES
DIETARY: Gluten-free, dairy-free, vegan

220 CALORIES, 5G PROTEIN, 40G CARBS, 5G FAT

INGREDIENTS:
- 1 cup basmati or jasmine rice
- 2 cups vegetable broth
- 1 tbsp olive oil
- 1 tsp ground cumin
- 1 tsp ground coriander
- ½ tsp turmeric
- ½ tsp cinnamon
- Salt and pepper to taste
- Fresh cilantro or parsley for garnish

INSTRUCTIONS:
1. Heat olive oil in a saucepan over medium heat. Add the cumin, coriander, turmeric, and cinnamon, and cook for 1 minute until fragrant.
2. Stir in the rice and coat it with the spices.
3. Add the vegetable broth and bring to a boil. Reduce heat to low, cover, and simmer for 15 minutes, or until the rice is fully cooked.
4. Fluff with a fork, season with salt and pepper, and garnish with fresh cilantro or parsley.

BATCH-COOKING TIP:
Make extra rice and store it in the fridge for up to 3 days. It reheats well and can be used as a side or base for other meals.

ROASTED SWEET POTATOES WITH ZA'ATAR

PREP TIME: 25 MINUTES
DIETARY: Gluten-free, dairy-free, vegan

200 CALORIES, 4G PROTEIN, 40G CARBS, 6G FAT

INGREDIENTS:
- 2 medium sweet potatoes (cut into wedges)
- 2 tbsp olive oil
- 1 tbsp za'atar seasoning
- Salt and pepper to taste
- Fresh parsley for garnish

INSTRUCTIONS:
1. Preheat the oven to 400°F (200°C).
2. In a large bowl, toss the sweet potato wedges with olive oil, za'atar, salt, and pepper.
3. Spread the sweet potatoes in a single layer on a baking sheet and roast for 25-30 minutes, flipping halfway through, until crispy and tender.
4. Garnish with fresh parsley and serve immediately.

BATCH-COOKING TIP:
Roast extra sweet potatoes and store them in the fridge for up to 3 days. They can be reheated or tossed into salads or grain bowls.

GRILLED POLENTA WITH HERBS

PREP TIME: 10 MINUTES
DIETARY: Gluten-free, dairy-free

10 CALORIES, 6G PROTEIN, 25G CARBS, 12G FAT

INGREDIENTS:

- 1 tube of pre-cooked polenta (sliced into rounds)
- 2 tbsp olive oil
- 1 tsp dried oregano
- 1 tsp dried thyme
- Salt and pepper to taste
- Fresh rosemary or basil for garnish

INSTRUCTIONS:

1. Preheat a grill pan over medium-high heat.
2. Brush the polenta slices with olive oil and season with oregano, thyme, salt, and pepper.
3. Grill the polenta rounds for 3-4 minutes on each side until golden and crispy.
4. Garnish with fresh herbs like rosemary or basil and serve warm.

BATCH-COOKING TIP: Grill extra polenta and store it in the fridge for up to 3 days. It can be reheated in a skillet or oven.

GREEK-STYLE GREEN BEANS (FASOLAKIA)

PREP TIME: 20 MINUTES
DIETARY: Gluten-free, dairy-free, vegan

150 CALORIES, 3G PROTEIN, 15G CARBS, 9G FAT

INGREDIENTS:

- 1 lb green beans (trimmed)
- 2 tbsp olive oil
- 1 small onion (chopped)
- 2 cloves garlic (minced)
- 1 can (14 oz) diced tomatoes
- 1 tsp dried oregano
- Salt and pepper to taste
- Fresh parsley for garnish

INSTRUCTIONS:

1. Heat olive oil in a large skillet over medium heat. Add the onion and garlic, and sauté for 3-4 minutes until softened.
2. Stir in the diced tomatoes, oregano, salt, and pepper. Cook for 5 minutes to let the flavors combine.
3. Add the green beans to the skillet, stir to coat with the tomato mixture, and cover. Cook for 10-12 minutes until the green beans are tender but still slightly crisp.
4. Garnish with fresh parsley and serve.

BATCH-COOKING TIP: Make extra green beans and store

them in the fridge for up to 3 days. They reheat well and can be served as a side or added to salads.

LEMON-GARLIC ROASTED CAULIFLOWER

PREP TIME: 20 MINUTES
DIETARY: Gluten-free, dairy-free, vegan

140 CALORIES, 3G PROTEIN, 15G CARBS, 8G FAT

INGREDIENTS:

- 1 medium head of cauliflower (cut into florets)
- 3 tbsp olive oil
- 3 cloves garlic (minced)
- Juice of 1 lemon
- 1 tsp paprika
- Salt and pepper to taste
- Fresh parsley for garnish

INSTRUCTIONS:

1. Preheat the oven to 400°F (200°C).
2. In a large bowl, toss the cauliflower florets with olive oil, garlic, lemon juice, paprika, salt, and pepper.
3. Spread the cauliflower in a single layer on a baking sheet.
4. Roast for 20-25 minutes, flipping halfway through, until golden and tender.

5. Garnish with fresh parsley and serve.

BATCH-COOKING TIP: Roast extra cauliflower and store i in the fridge for up to 3 days. Reheat or use it in grain bowls, salads, or wraps.

CHARRED BELL PEPPERS WITH FETA AND OLIVES

PREP TIME: 10 MINUTES
DIETARY: GLUTEN-FREE, DAIRY-FREE OPTION

180 CALORIES, 4G PROTEIN, 12G CARBS, 14G FAT

INGREDIENTS:

- 2 red bell peppers (cut into quarters)
- 2 tbsp olive oil
- ¼ cup crumbled feta (optional)
- ¼ cup Kalamata olives (halved)
- 1 tbsp fresh basil (chopped)
- Salt and pepper to taste

INSTRUCTIONS:

1. Preheat a grill or grill pan over medium-high heat
2. Brush the bell peppers with olive oil and season with salt and pepper.
3. Grill the peppers for 3-4 minutes on each side unti they are charred and softened.
4. Transfer the peppers to a serving plate and top with crumbled feta, Kalamata olives, and fresh basil.
5. Serve warm or at room temperature.

DAIRY-FREE: omit the feta or use a dairy-free cheese al ternative.

BATCH-COOKING TIP: Grill extra bell peppers and stor them in the fridge for up to 3 days. They can be used i sandwiches, wraps, or added to salads.

MEDITERRANEAN RICE PILAF

PREP TIME: 20 MINUTES
DIETARY: GLUTEN-FREE, DAIRY-FREE, VEGAn

210 CALORIES, 4G PROTEIN, 40G CARBS, 5G FAT

INGREDIENTS:

- 1 cup long-grain rice
- 2 tbsp olive oil
- 1 small onion (finely chopped)

- 2 cups vegetable broth
- ¼ cup slivered almonds (toasted)
- ¼ cup golden raisins
- 1 tsp ground cumin
- Salt and pepper to taste
- Fresh parsley for garnish

INSTRUCTIONS:

1. Heat olive oil in a large saucepan over medium heat. Add the onion and cook for 3-4 minutes until softened.
2. Stir in the rice and cumin, cooking for 1-2 minutes to toast the rice slightly.
3. Add the vegetable broth, bring to a boil, then reduce the heat to low. Cover and simmer for 15-18 minutes until the rice is tender and the liquid is absorbed.
4. Stir in the toasted almonds and golden raisins, and season with salt and pepper.
5. Garnish with fresh parsley and serve.

BATCH-COOKING TIP: Make extra rice pilaf and store it in the fridge for up to 3 days. It reheats well for quick meals.

ROASTED CARROTS WITH TAHINI DRIZZLE

PREP TIME: 25 MINUTES
DIETARY: GLUTEN-FREE, DAIRY-FREE, VEGAN

160 CALORIES, 2G PROTEIN, 20G CARBS, 10G FAT

INGREDIENTS:

- 6-8 medium carrots (peeled and halved lengthwise)
- 2 tbsp olive oil
- 1 tsp cumin
- Salt and pepper to taste
- Tahini Drizzle:
- 2 tbsp tahini
- Juice of ½ lemon
- 1 tbsp water
- Salt and pepper to taste

INSTRUCTIONS:

1. Preheat the oven to 400°F (200°C).
2. Toss the carrots with olive oil, cumin, salt, and pepper, and spread them on a baking sheet.
3. Roast for 25-30 minutes, flipping halfway through, until the carrots are tender and caramelized.

4. In a small bowl, whisk together the tahini, lemon juice, water, salt, and pepper to make the drizzle.
5. Drizzle the tahini sauce over the roasted carrots and serve.

BATCH-COOKING TIP: Roast extra carrots and store them in the fridge for up to 3 days. The tahini drizzle can also be made ahead and stored in the fridge.

BAKED EGGPLANT WITH GARLIC AND PARSLEY

PREP TIME: 25 MINUTES
DIETARY: GLUTEN-FREE, DAIRY-FREE, VEGAN

160 CALORIES, 3G PROTEIN, 18G CARBS, 9G FAT

INGREDIENTS:

- 1 large eggplant (sliced into rounds)
- 3 tbsp olive oil
- 2 cloves garlic (minced)
- 1 tsp dried oregano
- Salt and pepper to taste
- Fresh parsley for garnish

INSTRUCTIONS:

1. Preheat the oven to 400°F (200°C).
2. Brush the eggplant slices with olive oil on both sides and season with salt, pepper, oregano, and garlic.

3. Arrange the eggplant slices on a baking sheet and bake for 25-30 minutes, flipping halfway through, until golden and tender.
4. Garnish with fresh parsley and serve.

BATCH-COOKING TIP: Bake extra eggplant and store it in the fridge for up to 3 days. It can be reheated or used in sandwiches, wraps, or grain bowls.

SAUTÉED SPINACH WITH PINE NUTS AND RAISINS

PREP TIME: 10 MINUTES
DIETARY: GLUTEN-FREE, DAIRY-FREE, VEGAN

150 CALORIES, 4G PROTEIN, 12G CARBS, 11G FAT

INGREDIENTS:
- 2 tbsp olive oil
- 2 cloves garlic (minced)
- 6 cups fresh spinach
- 2 tbsp pine nuts (toasted)
- 2 tbsp raisins
- Salt and pepper to taste

INSTRUCTIONS:
1. Heat olive oil in a large skillet over medium heat. Add the garlic and sauté for 1-2 minutes until fragrant.
2. Stir in the spinach and cook until wilted, about 3-4 minutes.

3. Stir in the toasted pine nuts and raisins. Season with salt and pepper, and serve immediately.

BATCH-COOKING TIP: Sauté extra spinach and store it in the fridge for up to 2 days. It can be used in sandwiches, wraps, or tossed with pasta.

LEMON GARLIC GREEN BEANS

PREP TIME: 8 MINUTES
DIETARY: GLUTEN-FREE, DAIRY-FREE, VEGAN

80 CALORIES, 2G PROTEIN, 10G CARBS, 4G FAT

INGREDIENTS:
- 1 lb green beans (trimmed)
- 2 tbsp olive oil
- 2 cloves garlic (minced)
- Juice of 1 lemon
- Salt and pepper to taste

INSTRUCTIONS:
1. Heat olive oil in a large skillet over medium heat.
2. Add the garlic and sauté for 1 minute.
3. Add the green beans, season with salt and pepper, and sauté for 5-7 minutes until they're tender but still crisp.
4. Drizzle with lemon juice and serve immediately.

BATCH-COOKING TIP: Make extra green beans and store them in the fridge for up to 2 days. They're great reheated or tossed in salads.

GRILLED ASPARAGUS WITH LEMON AND PARMESAN

PREP TIME: 10 MINUTES
DIETARY: GLUTEN-FREE, DAIRY-FREE OPTION

120 CALORIES, 5G PROTEIN, 5G CARBS, 10G FAT

INGREDIENTS:
- 1 bunch of asparagus (trimmed)
- 2 tbsp olive oil
- Juice of 1 lemon
- ¼ cup shaved Parmesan (optional)
- Salt and pepper to taste

INSTRUCTIONS:
1. Preheat a grill or grill pan over medium-high heat.

2. Toss the asparagus with olive oil, lemon juice, salt, and pepper.
3. Grill the asparagus for 4-5 minutes, turning occasionally, until tender and charred.
4. Garnish with shaved Parmesan (if using) and serve.

DAIRY-FREE: Omit the Parmesan.

BATCH-COOKING TIP: Grill extra asparagus and store it in the fridge for up to 2 days. It's great in salads, grain bowls, or as a side dish.

2. Add the garlic and sauté for 1 minute until fragrant.
3. Add the zucchini slices, oregano, salt, and pepper. Sauté for 5-7 minutes until the zucchini is tender and slightly golden.
4. Garnish with fresh parsley and serve.

BATCH-COOKING TIP: Sauté extra zucchini and store in the fridge for up to 2 days. It can be used in wraps, grain bowls, or pasta.

QUICK SAUTÉED ZUCCHINI WITH GARLIC AND HERBS

PREP TIME: 10 MINUTES
DIETARY: GLUTEN-FREE, DAIRY-FREE, VEGAN

0 CALORIES, 2G PROTEIN, 8G CARBS, 6G FAT

INGREDIENTS:

2 medium zucchinis (sliced)
2 tbsp olive oil
2 cloves garlic (minced)
1 tsp dried oregano
Salt and pepper to taste
Fresh parsley for garnish

INSTRUCTIONS:

1. Heat olive oil in a large skillet over medium heat.

SALADS

CLASSIC GREEK SALAD WITH FETA AND OLIVES

PREP TIME: 10 MINUTES
DIETARY: GLUTEN-FREE, VEGETARIAN

200 CALORIES, 6G PROTEIN, 10G CARBS, 15G FAT

INGREDIENTS:
- 2 large tomatoes (chopped)
- 1 cucumber (sliced)
- 1 small red onion (thinly sliced)
- ¼ cup Kalamata olives (pitted)
- ¼ cup crumbled feta cheese
- 2 tbsp olive oil
- 1 tbsp red wine vinegar
- 1 tsp dried oregano
- Salt and pepper to taste

INSTRUCTIONS:
1. In a large bowl, combine the chopped tomatoes, cucumber, red onion, and olives.
2. Drizzle with olive oil and red wine vinegar, and sprinkle with dried oregano, salt, and pepper.
3. Toss to combine, then top with crumbled feta cheese. Serve immediately.

BATCH-COOKING TIP: Prep the veggies in advance and store them separately. Combine and dress right before serving for freshness.

SIMPLE TABBOULEH

PREP TIME: 15 MINUTES
DIETARY: VEGAN, DAIRY-FREE

180 CALORIES, 5G PROTEIN, 25G CARBS, 8G FAT

INGREDIENTS:
- 1 cup bulgur wheat
- 1 ¼ cups boiling water
- 1 bunch fresh parsley (finely chopped)
- ½ bunch fresh mint (chopped)
- 2 large tomatoes (diced)

- 1 small cucumber (diced)
- Juice of 1 lemon
- 3 tbsp olive oil
- Salt and pepper to taste

INSTRUCTIONS:

1. In a bowl, pour the boiling water over the bulgur wheat, cover, and let it sit for 5 minutes until softened.
2. Fluff the bulgur with a fork and add the chopped parsley, mint, tomatoes, and cucumber.
3. Drizzle with lemon juice, olive oil, and season with salt and pepper. Toss to combine and serve.

BATCH-COOKING TIP: Make extra bulgur and store it in the fridge for up to 3 days. You can toss it with veggies or use it as a base for other salads.

CHICKPEA SALAD WITH CUCUMBER AND LEMON

PREP TIME: 10 MINUTES
DIETARY: GLUTEN-FREE, DAIRY-FREE, VEGAN

220 CALORIES, 8G PROTEIN, 30G CARBS, 9G FAT

INGREDIENTS:

- 1 can (15 oz) chickpeas (drained and rinsed)
- 1 cucumber (diced)
- 1 small red onion (diced)
- 2 tbsp olive oil
- Juice of 1 lemon
- 1 tbsp fresh parsley (chopped)
- Salt and pepper to taste

INSTRUCTIONS:

1. In a large bowl, combine the chickpeas, cucumber, and red onion.
2. Drizzle with olive oil and lemon juice, and season with salt, pepper, and fresh parsley.
3. Toss to combine and serve immediately or chill for a refreshing side.

BATCH-COOKING TIP: Make extra chickpea salad and store it in the fridge for up to 3 days. It can be used in wraps or as a filling for pita.

HERBED QUINOA SALAD WITH ASPARAGUS AND PEAS

PREP TIME: 10 MINUTES
DIETARY: GLUTEN-FREE, DAIRY-FREE, VEGAN

290 CALORIES, 8G PROTEIN, 40G CARBS, 10G FAT

INGREDIENTS:

- 1 cup quinoa (rinsed)
- 2 cups water or vegetable broth
- 1 cup fresh or frozen peas
- 1 bunch asparagus (trimmed and cut into 2-inch pieces)
- 2 tbsp olive oil
- Juice of 1 lemon
- Zest of 1 lemon

- 2 tbsp fresh parsley (chopped)
- Salt and pepper to taste

INSTRUCTIONS:

1. In a saucepan, bring the quinoa and water (or broth) to a boil. Reduce heat and simmer for 10 minutes until the quinoa is cooked and the water is absorbed. Fluff with a fork.
2. While the quinoa is cooking, bring a pot of salted water to a boil. Blanch the asparagus and peas for 2-3 minutes until just tender but still crisp. Drain and immediately transfer them to an ice bath to stop the cooking process.

3. Once the quinoa is ready, combine it with the blanched asparagus and peas in a large bowl.
4. Drizzle with olive oil and lemon juice, then add the lemon zest and chopped parsley.
5. Season with salt and pepper, toss to combine, and serve immediately.

BATCH-COOKING TIP: Make extra quinoa salad and store it in the fridge for up to 3 days. It can be served cold as a refreshing side or tossed with greens for a light lunch.

MEDITERRANEAN LENTIL SALAD WITH RED ONION AND PARSLEY

PREP TIME: 10 MINUTES
DIETARY: GLUTEN-FREE, DAIRY-FREE, VEGAN

200 CALORIES, 12G PROTEIN, 30G CARBS, 5G FAT

INGREDIENTS:

* 1 cup cooked lentils (or canned, drained and rinsed)
* ½ small red onion (finely chopped)
* 1 tbsp olive oil
* Juice of 1 lemon
* 2 tbsp fresh parsley (chopped)
* Salt and pepper to taste

INSTRUCTIONS:

1. In a large bowl, combine the cooked lentils, red onion, and parsley.
2. Drizzle with olive oil and lemon juice, and season with salt and pepper.
3. Toss to combine and serve.

BATCH-COOKING TIP: Make extra lentil salad and store in the fridge for up to 3 days. It's great for quick lunches or a filling for pita wraps.

ORZO SALAD WITH SPINACH AND SUN-DRIED TOMATOES

PREP TIME: 15 MINUTES
DIETARY: VEGETARIAN, DAIRY-FREE OPTION

250 CALORIES, 8G PROTEIN, 35G CARBS, 9G FAT

INGREDIENTS:

* 1 cup orzo (or gluten-free pasta)
* 2 cups fresh spinach (chopped)
* ¼ cup sun-dried tomatoes (chopped)
* 2 tbsp olive oil
* Juice of 1 lemon
* ¼ cup crumbled feta (optional)
* Salt and pepper to taste

INSTRUCTIONS:

1. Cook the orzo according to package instructions. Drain and set aside.
2. In a large bowl, combine the cooked orzo with chopped spinach and sun-dried tomatoes.
3. Drizzle with olive oil and lemon juice, and season with salt and pepper.
4. Toss to combine and top with crumbled feta (if using). Serve warm or cold.

BATCH-COOKING TIP: Make extra orzo salad and store it in the fridge for up to 3 days. It can be served as a cold pasta salad or a quick side.

SHAVED CUCUMBER AND DILL SALAD

PREP TIME: 5 MINUTES
PREP TIME: NONE
DIETARY: GLUTEN-FREE, DAIRY-FREE, VEGAN

90 CALORIES, 2G PROTEIN, 10G CARBS, 5G FAT

INGREDIENTS:

- 2 large cucumbers (thinly sliced or shaved with a peeler)
- 2 tbsp olive oil
- 2 tbsp white wine vinegar
- 1 tbsp fresh dill (chopped)
- Salt and pepper to taste

INSTRUCTIONS:

1. In a large bowl, combine the shaved cucumber slices with olive oil, vinegar, and dill.
2. Season with salt and pepper, then toss to combine.
3. Serve immediately for a crisp, refreshing side.

BATCH-COOKING TIP: Make extra cucumber salad and store it in the fridge for up to 2 days. This salad is best eaten fresh but can still hold up well when chilled.

WATERMELON AND FETA SALAD WITH MINT

PREP TIME: 5 MINUTES
DIETARY: GLUTEN-FREE, VEGETARIAN

180 CALORIES, 4G PROTEIN, 18G CARBS, 8G FAT

INGREDIENTS:

- 2 cups watermelon (cubed)
- ¼ cup crumbled feta cheese

- 2 tbsp fresh mint (chopped)
- 1 tbsp olive oil
- 1 tbsp balsamic vinegar (optional)
- Salt and pepper to taste

INSTRUCTIONS:

1. In a large bowl, combine the watermelon cubes with crumbled feta and fresh mint.
2. Drizzle with olive oil and balsamic vinegar (if using), then season with a pinch of salt and pepper.
3. Toss gently to combine and serve immediately.

BATCH-COOKING TIP: Watermelon salad is best served fresh, but you can cube the watermelon ahead of time and store it in the fridge for up to 2 days.

ROASTED RED PEPPER AND FETA SALAD

PREP TIME: 5 MINUTES
DIETARY: GLUTEN-FREE, VEGETARIAN

180 CALORIES, 6G PROTEIN, 8G CARBS, 14G FAT

INGREDIENTS:

- 1 jar (12 oz) roasted red peppers (drained and sliced)
- ¼ cup crumbled feta
- 1 tbsp olive oil

- 1 tbsp balsamic vinegar
- 1 tsp dried oregano
- Salt and pepper to taste

INSTRUCTIONS:

1. In a bowl, combine the roasted red pepper slices and crumbled feta.
2. Drizzle with olive oil and balsamic vinegar, then sprinkle with oregano, salt, and pepper.
3. Toss gently to combine and serve.

BATCH-COOKING TIP: Make extra roasted red pepper salad and store it in the fridge for up to 3 days. It can also be used as a topping for grilled meats or sandwiches.
4.

POMEGRANATE, ARUGULA AND WALNUTS SALAD

PREP TIME: 5 MINUTES
DIETARY: GLUTEN-FREE, DAIRY-FREE, VEGAN

180 CALORIES, 4G PROTEIN, 12G CARBS, 14G FAT

INGREDIENTS:

- 2 cups arugula
- ¼ cup pomegranate seeds
- ¼ cup walnuts (chopped)
- 2 tbsp olive oil

- Juice of ½ lemon
- Salt and pepper to taste

INSTRUCTIONS:

1. In a large bowl, combine the arugula, pomegranate seeds, and chopped walnuts.
2. Drizzle with olive oil and lemon juice, then season with salt and pepper.
3. Toss to combine and serve.

BATCH-COOKING TIP: Make extra arugula salad and store it in the fridge for up to 2 days. Keep the dressing separate until ready to serve for best results.

ZESTY CARROT AND CABBAGE SLAW

PREP TIME: 10 MINUTES
DIETARY: GLUTEN-FREE, DAIRY-FREE, VEGAN

110 CALORIES, 2G PROTEIN, 12G CARBS, 7G FAT

INGREDIENTS:

- 2 cups shredded cabbage
- 1 large carrot (grated)
- 2 tbsp olive oil
- 2 tbsp apple cider vinegar
- 1 tsp Dijon mustard
- 1 tsp honey (optional for vegan)
- Salt and pepper to taste

INSTRUCTIONS:

1. In a large bowl, combine the shredded cabbage and grated carrot.
2. In a small bowl, whisk together the olive oil, apple cider vinegar, Dijon mustard, honey (if using), salt and pepper.
3. Pour the dressing over the vegetables and toss to combine.
4. Serve immediately or chill for later.

HEALTHY EATING REMINDERS

As you explore these Mediterranean recipes, remember that healthy eating is about balance, enjoyment, and sustainability. Here are a few simple reminders to keep in mind:

LISTEN TO YOUR BODY: Eat until you're satisfied, not stuffed. Mediterranean eating encourages mindfulness—take your time to enjoy the flavors and textures of your meals.

PORTION CONTROL MATTERS: It's not just about what you eat, but how much. These recipes are designed with balanced portions in mind, so you can nourish your body without overindulging.

VARIETY IS KEY: The Mediterranean diet is all about variety. Make sure your plate is colorful with plenty of fruits, vegetables, lean proteins, and healthy fats. The more diverse your meals, the more nutrients you'll get.

STAY HYDRATED: Water is essential! Aim to drink water throughout the day, and if you choose to drink wine with your meals, do so in moderation.

ENJOY THE EXPERIENCE: Mediterranean meals are meant to be shared. Whether you're eating with family, friends, or on your own, take time to enjoy the process of cooking and the joy of a wholesome, flavorful meal.

SOUPS

LEMON CHICKPEA SOUP WITH DILL

PREP TIME: 15 MINUTES
DIETARY: GLUTEN-FREE, DAIRY-FREE, VEGAN

220 CALORIES, 10G PROTEIN, 30G CARBS, 7G FAT

INGREDIENTS:

- 1 can (15 oz) chickpeas (drained and rinsed)
- 1 small onion (finely chopped)
- 2 tbsp olive oil
- 2 cloves garlic (minced)
- 4 cups vegetable broth
- Juice and zest of 1 lemon
- 2 tbsp fresh dill (chopped)
- Salt and pepper to taste

INSTRUCTIONS:

1. Heat olive oil in a pot over medium heat. Add the chopped onion and garlic, sautéing for 3-4 minutes until softened.
2. Add the chickpeas and vegetable broth, and bring to a boil. Lower the heat and let it simmer for 10 minutes.
3. Stir in the lemon juice, zest, and fresh dill. Season with salt and pepper to taste.
4. Serve with extra dill and a drizzle of olive oil.

BATCH-COOKING TIP:

Make extra chickpea soup and store it in the fridge for up to 3 days. It reheats well and can be served over rice or pasta for a more filling meal.

CREAMY ROASTED RED PEPPER AND WHITE BEAN SOUP

PREP TIME: 15 MINUTES
DIETARY: GLUTEN-FREE, DAIRY-FREE, VEGAN

240 CALORIES, 9G PROTEIN, 35G CARBS, 8G FAT

INGREDIENTS:

- 1 jar (12 oz) roasted red peppers (drained)
- 1 can (15 oz) white beans (drained and rinsed)
- 1 small onion (chopped)
- 2 cloves garlic (minced)
- 2 tbsp olive oil
- 4 cups vegetable broth
- 1 tsp smoked paprika
- 2 tbsp fresh parsley (chopped)
- Salt and pepper to taste

INSTRUCTIONS:

1. Heat olive oil in a pot over medium heat. Add the chopped onion and garlic, and sauté for 3-4 minutes until softened.
2. Add the roasted red peppers, white beans, vegetable broth, and smoked paprika. Bring to a boil, then lower the heat and simmer for 10 minutes.
3. Use an immersion blender to blend the soup until smooth.
4. Season with salt and pepper, and garnish with fresh parsley before serving.

BATCH-COOKING TIP: Make extra roasted red pepper soup and store it in the fridge for up to 3 days. Reheat and serve with crusty bread or over cooked grains.

SPICED CARROT AND LENTIL SOUP WITH HARISSA

PREP TIME: 15 MINUTES
DIETARY: GLUTEN-FREE, DAIRY-FREE, VEGAN

30 CALORIES, 12G PROTEIN, 30G CARBS, 8G FAT

INGREDIENTS:

2 medium carrots (peeled and chopped)
½ cup red lentils
1 small onion (chopped)
2 tbsp olive oil
1 tbsp harissa paste
4 cups vegetable broth
1 tsp ground cumin
Salt and pepper to taste
Fresh cilantro for garnish

INSTRUCTIONS:

Heat olive oil in a pot over medium heat. Add the chopped onion and carrots, and sauté for 5 minutes until the vegetables are softened.

Stir in the harissa, cumin, and red lentils, and cook for 1 minute.

3. Add the vegetable broth, bring to a boil, then lower the heat and simmer for 10-12 minutes until the lentils are cooked.

4. Blend half the soup with an immersion blender for a creamier texture, then season with salt and pepper. Garnish with fresh cilantro.

BATCH-COOKING TIP: Make extra carrot and lentil soup and store it in the fridge for up to 3 days. It thickens as it sits, so it can also be used as a dip or spread.

ZUCCHINI AND FENNEL SOUP WITH FRESH MINT

PREP TIME: 12 MINUTES
DIETARY: GLUTEN-FREE, DAIRY-FREE, VEGAN

190 CALORIES, 4G PROTEIN, 18G CARBS, 10G FAT

INGREDIENTS:

- 2 medium zucchinis (chopped)
- 1 small fennel bulb (sliced)
- 2 tbsp olive oil
- 1 small onion (chopped)
- 4 cups vegetable broth
- 1 tsp ground coriander
- 2 tbsp fresh mint (chopped)
- Salt and pepper to taste

INSTRUCTIONS:

1. Heat olive oil in a pot over medium heat. Add the onion, zucchini, and fennel, and sauté for 5 minutes until softened.
2. Stir in the ground coriander, then add the vegetable broth. Bring to a boil, then simmer for 7-8 minutes until the vegetables are tender.
3. Use an immersion blender to blend the soup until smooth. Season with salt and pepper, and garnish with fresh mint.

BATCH-COOKING TIP: Make extra zucchini soup and store it in the fridge for up to 3 days. Serve it hot or chilled for a refreshing summer dish.

GARLIC AND HERB ORZO SOUP WITH SPINACH

PREP TIME: 15 MINUTES
DIETARY: VEGETARIAN, DAIRY-FREE OPTION

210 CALORIES, 8G PROTEIN, 35G CARBS, 5G FAT

INGREDIENTS:

- ½ cup orzo pasta
- 2 tbsp olive oil
- 3 cloves garlic (minced)
- 4 cups vegetable broth
- 2 cups fresh spinach (chopped)
- 1 tsp dried oregano
- Salt and pepper to taste
- Fresh Parmesan (optional, for garnish)

INSTRUCTIONS:

1. Heat olive oil in a pot over medium heat. Add the minced garlic and sauté for 1 minute until fragrant.
2. Add the orzo, vegetable broth, and oregano. Bring to a boil and cook for 8-10 minutes until the orzo is tender.
3. Stir in the chopped spinach and season with salt and pepper. Garnish with Parmesan if desired.

BATCH-COOKING TIP: Make extra orzo soup and store it in the fridge for up to 2 days. It thickens as it sits, so you can add extra broth when reheating.

GREEK EGGPLANT AND TOMATO SOUP WITH OLIVE OIL DRIZZLE

PREP TIME: 15 MINUTES
DIETARY: GLUTEN-FREE, DAIRY-FREE, VEGAN

210 CALORIES, 5G PROTEIN, 25G CARBS, 12G FAT

INGREDIENTS:

- 1 medium eggplant (peeled and diced)
- 1 can (14 oz) diced tomatoes
- 2 tbsp olive oil (plus extra for drizzling)
- 1 small onion (chopped)
- 2 cloves garlic (minced)
- 4 cups vegetable broth
- 1 tsp dried oregano
- Salt and pepper to taste
- Fresh basil for garnish

INSTRUCTIONS:

1. Heat olive oil in a pot over medium heat. Add the chopped onion, garlic, and eggplant, and sauté for 5 minutes until softened.
2. Add the diced tomatoes, oregano, and vegetable broth. Bring to a boil, then simmer for 10 minutes until the eggplant is tender.
3. Use an immersion blender to blend the soup until smooth. Season with salt and pepper, drizzle with extra olive oil, and garnish with fresh basil before serving.

BATCH-COOKING TIP: Make extra eggplant and tomato soup and store it in the fridge for up to 3 days. Reheat and serve with toasted pita or crusty bread.

QUICK TOMATO, FETA, AND OLIVE SOUP

PREP TIME: 15 MINUTES
DIETARY: GLUTEN-FREE, VEGETARIAN

220 CALORIES, 7G PROTEIN, 18G CARBS, 14G FAT

INGREDIENTS:

- 1 can (14 oz) diced tomatoes
- 1 small onion (chopped)
- 2 cloves garlic (minced)
- 2 tbsp olive oil
- ¼ cup Kalamata olives (pitted and chopped)
- ¼ cup crumbled feta cheese
- 4 cups vegetable broth
- 1 tsp dried oregano
- Salt and pepper to taste

INSTRUCTIONS:

1. Heat olive oil in a pot over medium heat. Add the onion and garlic, and sauté for 3-4 minutes until softened.
2. Add the diced tomatoes, vegetable broth, olives, and oregano. Bring to a boil and simmer for 10 minutes.
3. Stir in the crumbled feta and season with salt and pepper before serving.

BATCH-COOKING TIP: Make extra tomato soup and store in the fridge for up to 3 days. It can also be used as a sauce over pasta or grains.

CHILLED CUCUMBER AND YOGURT SOUP WITH DILL

PREP TIME: 15 MINUTES
DIETARY: GLUTEN-FREE, VEGETARIAN, DAIRY-FREE OPTION

140 CALORIES, 6G PROTEIN, 10G CARBS, 8G FAT

INGREDIENTS:

- 2 large cucumbers (peeled and chopped)
- 1 cup plain Greek yogurt (or dairy-free yogurt)
- 2 tbsp fresh dill (chopped)
- 2 tbsp olive oil
- Juice of 1 lemon
- Salt and pepper to taste

INSTRUCTIONS:

1. In a blender, combine the chopped cucumbers, yogurt, dill, olive oil, and lemon juice. Blend until smooth.
2. Season with salt and pepper, and chill the soup in the fridge for 10 minutes before serving.
3. Serve cold, garnished with extra dill and a drizzle of olive oil.

BATCH-COOKING TIP: Make extra cucumber soup and store it in the fridge for up to 2 days. Perfect for a refreshing appetizer or light lunch.

SAFFRON AND CHICKPEA SOUP WITH LEMON

PREP TIME: 15 MINUTES
DIETARY: GLUTEN-FREE, DAIRY-FREE, VEGAN

230 CALORIES, 9G PROTEIN, 30G CARBS, 9G FAT

INGREDIENTS:

- 1 can (15 oz) chickpeas (drained and rinsed)
- 1 small onion (chopped)
- 2 cloves garlic (minced)
- 2 tbsp olive oil
- 4 cups vegetable broth

- ¼ tsp saffron threads (optional, for added depth)
- Juice of 1 lemon
- Salt and pepper to taste
- Fresh parsley for garnish

INSTRUCTIONS:

1. Heat olive oil in a pot over medium heat. Add the onion and garlic, and sauté for 3-4 minutes until softened.
2. Add the chickpeas, saffron (if using), and vegetable broth. Bring to a boil and simmer for 10 minutes.
3. Stir in the lemon juice, season with salt and pepper, and garnish with fresh parsley before serving.

BATCH-COOKING TIP: Make extra chickpea soup and store it in the fridge for up to 3 days. Reheat and serve with pita bread or rice for a heartier meal.

CAULIFLOWER AND TAHINI SOUP WITH PINE NUTS

PREP TIME: 15 MINUTES
DIETARY: GLUTEN-FREE, DAIRY-FREE, VEGAN

210 CALORIES, 7G PROTEIN, 18G CARBS, 13G FAT

INGREDIENTS:

- 1 small head of cauliflower (cut into florets)
- 2 tbsp tahini
- 1 small onion (chopped)
- 2 cloves garlic (minced)
- 2 tbsp olive oil
- 4 cups vegetable broth
- ¼ cup pine nuts (toasted)
- Salt and pepper to taste

INSTRUCTIONS:

1. Heat olive oil in a pot over medium heat. Add the onion, garlic, and cauliflower, and sauté for 5 minutes until softened.
2. Add the vegetable broth and bring to a boil. Simmer for 10 minutes until the cauliflower is tender.
3. Stir in the tahini, then use an immersion blender to blend the soup until smooth.
4. Season with salt and pepper, and garnish with toasted pine nuts before serving.

BATCH-COOKING TIP:
Make extra cauliflower soup and store in the fridge for up to 3 days. Reheat and serve with a drizzle of extra tahini.

QUICK LEMON GARLIC SHRIMP SOUP

PREP TIME: 15 MINUTES
DIETARY: GLUTEN-FREE, DAIRY-FREE

200 CALORIES, 18G PROTEIN, 8G CARBS, 9G FAT

INGREDIENTS:

- 200g shrimp (peeled and deveined)
- 2 cloves garlic (minced)
- 2 tbsp olive oil
- 4 cups vegetable broth
- Juice and zest of 1 lemon
- 1 tsp dried oregano
- 2 tbsp fresh parsley (chopped)
- Salt and pepper to taste

INSTRUCTIONS:

1. Heat olive oil in a pot over medium heat. Add the minced garlic and sauté for 1 minute until fragrant.
2. Add the vegetable broth, lemon zest, and oregano. Bring to a boil and simmer for 5 minutes.
3. Add the shrimp and cook for 3-4 minutes until they turn pink and are fully cooked.
4. Stir in the lemon juice, season with salt and pepper, and garnish with fresh parsley before serving.

BATCH-COOKING TIP: Make extra broth and add the shrimp right before serving. The soup broth can be stored for 2 days in the fridge and quickly reheated with the shrimp.

LITE BITES

BAKED FALAFEL WITH TAHINI DIP

COOK TIME: 20 MINUTES
DIETARY: GLUTEN-FREE, DAIRY-FREE, VEGAN

0 CALORIES, 8G PROTEIN, 25G CARBS, 8G FAT

INGREDIENTS:

- 1 can (15 oz) chickpeas (drained and rinsed)
- 1 small onion (chopped)
- 2 cloves garlic (minced)
- 2 tbsp fresh parsley (chopped)
- 1 tsp ground cumin
- 1 tsp ground coriander
- 2 tbsp olive oil
- 2 tbsp chickpea flour (or all-purpose flour)
- Salt and pepper to taste
- Tahini Dip:
- 2 tbsp tahini
- Juice of ½ lemon
- 1 tbsp olive oil
- Water to thin
- Salt and pepper to taste

INSTRUCTIONS:

1. Preheat the oven to 400°F (200°C) and line a baking sheet with parchment paper.
2. In a food processor, combine the chickpeas, onion, garlic, parsley, cumin, coriander, olive oil, chickpea flour, salt, and pepper. Pulse until the mixture forms a rough paste.
3. Scoop tablespoon-sized portions and shape them into small patties. Place them on the baking sheet.
4. Bake for 20 minutes, flipping halfway through, until golden and crispy.
5. While the falafel bakes, whisk together the tahini, lemon juice, olive oil, and water to make the dip. Season with salt and pepper.
6. Serve the falafel with the tahini dip.

BATCH-COOKING TIP: Make extra falafel and store them in the fridge for up to 3 days. They can be reheated or served cold in wraps or salads.

SPICED SWEET POTATO FRIES WITH GARLIC YOGURT DIP

COOK TIME: 20 MINUTES
DIETARY: GLUTEN-FREE, VEGETARIAN, DAIRY-FREE OPTION

220 CALORIES, 4G PROTEIN, 35G CARBS, 8G FAT

INGREDIENTS:

- 2 medium sweet potatoes (cut into fries)
- 2 tbsp olive oil
- 1 tsp smoked paprika
- 1 tsp ground cumin
- Salt and pepper to taste
- Garlic Yogurt Dip:
- ¼ cup Greek yogurt (or dairy-free yogurt)
- 1 clove garlic (minced)
- Juice of ½ lemon
- Salt and pepper to taste

INSTRUCTIONS:

1. Preheat the oven to 425°F (220°C).
2. Toss the sweet potato fries with olive oil, smoked paprika, cumin, salt, and pepper. Spread them in a single layer on a baking sheet.
3. Bake for 20 minutes, flipping halfway through, until crispy.
4. Meanwhile, whisk together the yogurt, garlic, lemon juice, salt, and pepper to make the dip.
5. Serve the sweet potato fries with the garlic yogurt dip.

BATCH-COOKING TIP: Make extra fries and store them in the fridge for up to 2 days. They can be reheated in the oven for crispiness.

QUICK MARINATED FETA-STUFFED MINI PEPPERS

PREP TIME: 15 MINUTES
DIETARY: GLUTEN-FREE, VEGETARIAN

160 CALORIES, 5G PROTEIN, 10G CARBS, 12G FAT

INGREDIENTS:

- 10-12 mini bell peppers (halved and seeded)
- ¼ cup crumbled feta
- 2 tbsp olive oil
- 1 tsp dried oregano
- 1 clove garlic (minced)
- Juice of ½ lemon
- Salt and pepper to taste
- Fresh parsley for garnish

INSTRUCTIONS:

1. In a small bowl, mix the crumbled feta, olive oil, oregano, garlic, lemon juice, salt, and pepper. Let it marinate for 5-10 minutes.
2. Stuff each mini bell pepper half with the marinated feta mixture.
3. Garnish with fresh parsley and serve immediately or let the flavors meld for 10 minutes in the fridge for a deeper taste.

BATCH-COOKING TIP: Make extra stuffed peppers and store them in the fridge for up to 2 days. They make for a perfect light snack or addition to a mezze platter

ROASTED RED PEPPER HUMMUS

PREP TIME: 5 MINUTES
DIETARY: GLUTEN-FREE, DAIRY-FREE, VEGAN

180 CALORIES, 6G PROTEIN, 15G CARBS, 10G FAT

INGREDIENTS:

- 1 can (15 oz) chickpeas (drained and rinsed)

- 1 jar (12 oz) roasted red peppers (drained)
- 2 tbsp tahini
- 2 tbsp olive oil
- 2 cloves garlic (minced)
- Juice of 1 lemon
- Salt and pepper to taste

INSTRUCTIONS:

1. In a food processor, combine the chickpeas, roasted red peppers, tahini, olive oil, garlic, and lemon juice.
2. Blend until smooth, adding a little water if needed for the desired consistency.
3. Season with salt and pepper to taste.
4. Serve with pita chips, veggies, or crackers.

BATCH-COOKING TIP: Make extra hummus and store it in the fridge for up to 5 days.

ZUCCHINI FRITTERS WITH TZATZIKI

PREP TIME: 15 MINUTES
DIETARY: GLUTEN-FREE, VEGETARIAN

200 CALORIES, 7G PROTEIN, 12G CARBS, 14G FAT

INGREDIENTS:

- 2 medium zucchinis (grated)
- ¼ cup flour (or gluten-free flour)

- 1 egg
- 2 tbsp fresh parsley (chopped)
- 1 clove garlic (minced)
- 2 tbsp olive oil
- Salt and pepper to taste
- Tzatziki:
- ½ cup Greek yogurt
- 1 small cucumber (grated)
- 1 clove garlic (minced)
- Juice of ½ lemon
- Salt and pepper to taste

INSTRUCTIONS:

1. Squeeze the excess water from the grated zucchini. In a bowl, combine the zucchini, flour, egg, parsley, garlic, salt, and pepper.
2. Heat olive oil in a skillet over medium heat. Drop spoonfuls of the mixture into the skillet and flatten slightly. Cook for 2-3 minutes on each side until golden and crispy.
3. Meanwhile, mix the tzatziki ingredients in a bowl.
4. Serve the fritters hot with tzatziki.

BATCH-COOKING TIP: Make extra fritters and store them in the fridge for up to 3 days. Reheat in the oven for crispiness.

MINI PITA PIZZAS WITH FETA AND OLIVES

PREP TIME: 15 MINUTES
DIETARY: VEGETARIAN

250 CALORIES, 10G PROTEIN, 30G CARBS, 12G FAT

INGREDIENTS:

- 4 mini pita breads
- ½ cup crumbled feta
- ¼ cup Kalamata olives (sliced)
- ½ cup marinara sauce
1 tbsp fresh oregano (chopped)

- Olive oil for drizzling

INSTRUCTIONS:

1. Preheat the oven to 400°F (200°C).
2. Spread a spoonful of marinara sauce on each pita bread.
3. Top with crumbled feta, sliced olives, and fresh oregano. Drizzle with a little olive oil.

4. Bake for 8-10 minutes until the edges are crispy and the cheese is slightly melted.
5. Serve immediately.

BATCH-COOKING TIP: Make extra pita pizzas and store them in the fridge for up to 2 days. Reheat in the oven to crisp up before serving.

SPINACH AND FETA PHYLLO ROLLS

PREP TIME: 10 MINUTES
DIETARY: VEGETARIAN

230 CALORIES, 7G PROTEIN, 30G CARBS, 10G FAT

INGREDIENTS:

- 1 cup fresh spinach (chopped)
- ¼ cup crumbled feta
- 6 sheets of phyllo dough
- 2 tbsp olive oil
- Salt and pepper to taste

INSTRUCTIONS:

1. Preheat the oven to 375°F (190°C).
2. In a bowl, combine the spinach, feta, salt, and pepper.
3. Lay out a sheet of phyllo dough, brush lightly with olive oil, and place another sheet on top. Repeat for a total of 3 sheets.
4. Place a spoonful of the spinach-feta mixture along one edge of the phyllo dough. Roll up and brush the top with olive oil.
5. Bake for 10 minutes until golden and crispy.

BATCH-COOKING TIP: Make extra rolls and store them in the fridge for up to 3 days. Reheat them in the oven for crispness.

GRILLED HALLOUMI WITH HONEY AND THYME

PREP TIME: 10 MINUTES
DIETARY: GLUTEN-FREE, VEGETARIAN

240 CALORIES, 14G PROTEIN, 6G CARBS, 18G FAT

INGREDIENTS:

- 200g halloumi cheese (sliced)
- 1 tbsp olive oil
- 1 tbsp honey
- 1 tsp fresh thyme (chopped)

INSTRUCTIONS:

6. Heat a grill pan over medium-high heat.
7. Brush the halloumi slices with olive oil and grill for 2-3 minutes on each side until golden.
8. Drizzle with honey and sprinkle with fresh thyme.
9. Serve immediately.

BATCH-COOKING TIP:
Halloumi is best served fresh, but leftovers can be reheated in a skillet.

EGGPLANT CAPONATA CROSTINI

PREP TIME: 10 MINUTES

DIETARY: GLUTEN-FREE OPTION, VEGAN

180 CALORIES, 4G PROTEIN, 22G CARBS, 10G FAT

INGREDIENTS:

- 1 small eggplant (diced)
- 2 tbsp olive oil
- 1 small onion (chopped)

- 1 tbsp capers
- 1 tbsp balsamic vinegar
- ½ tsp dried oregano
- 1 tbsp chopped parsley
- Salt and pepper to taste
- Baguette slices (or gluten-free crackers)

INSTRUCTIONS:

1. Heat olive oil in a skillet over medium heat. Add the onion and diced eggplant, cooking for 7-8 minutes until softened.
2. Stir in the capers, balsamic vinegar, oregano, salt, and pepper. Cook for an additional 2 minutes until the flavors meld.
3. Top baguette slices with the eggplant caponata and garnish with chopped parsley. Serve warm.

BATCH-COOKING TIP: Make extra caponata and store it in the fridge for up to 3 days. Serve it over toast, pasta, or as a side dish.

EGGPLANT BRUSCHETTA WITH TOMATOES AND BASIL

PREP TIME: 15 MINUTES
DIETARY: GLUTEN-FREE, VEGAN

190 CALORIES, 3G PROTEIN, 15G CARBS, 7G FAT

INGREDIENTS:

- 1 medium eggplant (sliced)
- 1 cup cherry tomatoes (halved)
- 1 clove garlic (minced)
- 2 tbsp olive oil
- 1 tbsp fresh basil (chopped)
- Salt and pepper to taste

INSTRUCTIONS:

1. Heat olive oil in a skillet over medium-high heat. Add the eggplant slices and cook for 3-4 minutes on each side until golden.
2. In a bowl, toss the tomatoes with garlic, olive oil, basil, salt, and pepper.
3. Top the eggplant slices with the tomato mixture and serve warm.

BATCH-COOKING TIP: Make extra bruschetta and store the tomato mixture separately in the fridge for up to 3 days.

CRISPY CHICKPEAS WITH PAPRIKA AND CUMIN

PREP TIME: 15 MINUTES
DIETARY: GLUTEN-FREE, DAIRY-FREE, VEGAN

160 CALORIES, 6G PROTEIN, 22G CARBS, 6G FAT

INGREDIENTS:

- 1 can (15 oz) chickpeas (drained and rinsed)
- 1 tbsp olive oil
- 1 tsp smoked paprika
- 1 tsp ground cumin
- Salt and pepper to taste

INSTRUCTIONS:

1. Preheat the oven to 400°F (200°C).
2. Pat the chickpeas dry and toss them with olive oil, paprika, cumin, salt, and pepper.
3. Spread the chickpeas on a baking sheet in a single layer and roast for 10-12 minutes until crispy.
4. Serve as a snack or salad topping.

BATCH-COOKING TIP: Make extra crispy chickpeas and store them in an airtight container for up to 3 days.

LEMON AND HERB MARINATED OLIVES

PREP TIME: 15 MINUTES
DIETARY: GLUTEN-FREE, DAIRY-FREE, VEGAN

140 CALORIES, 1G PROTEIN, 4G CARBS, 14G FAT

INGREDIENTS:

- 1 cup mixed olives (green and Kalamata)
- 2 tbsp olive oil
- Juice of ½ lemon
- 1 clove garlic (minced)
- 1 tbsp fresh parsley (chopped)
- 1 tsp dried oregano

INSTRUCTIONS:

1. In a bowl, combine the olives, olive oil, lemon juice, garlic, parsley, and oregano.
2. Toss to combine and let the olives marinate for at least 10 minutes.

3. Serve as a snack or appetizer.

BATCH-COOKING TIP: Make extra marinated olives and store them in the fridge for up to 1 week.

MEDITERRANEAN TUNA SALAD LETTUCE WRAPS

PREP TIME: 5 MINUTES
DIETARY: GLUTEN-FREE, DAIRY-FREE

180 CALORIES, 15G PROTEIN, 6G CARBS, 10G FAT

INGREDIENTS:

- 1 can (5 oz) tuna in olive oil (drained)
- 1 tbsp olive oil
- 1 tbsp fresh parsley (chopped)
- 1 tbsp capers (drained)
- Juice of ½ lemon
- 4 large lettuce leaves

INSTRUCTIONS:

1. In a bowl, combine the tuna, olive oil, parsley, capers, and lemon juice.
2. Spoon the tuna mixture into the lettuce leaves and serve as wraps.

BATCH-COOKING TIP: Make extra tuna salad and store it in the fridge for up to 2 days. Assemble wraps just before serving.

CUCUMBER BITES WITH HUMMUS AND SUN-DRIED TOMATOES

PREP TIME: 5 MINUTES
DIETARY: GLUTEN-FREE, DAIRY-FREE, VEGAN

90 CALORIES, 3G PROTEIN, 8G CARBS, 5G FAT

INGREDIENTS:

- 1 cucumber (sliced into rounds)
- ¼ cup hummus
- 2 tbsp sun-dried tomatoes (chopped)
- Fresh parsley for garnish

INSTRUCTIONS:

1. Spread a dollop of hummus on each cucumber slice.

2. Top with chopped sun-dried tomatoes and garnish with parsley.
3. Serve immediately.

BATCH-COOKING TIP: Make extra cucumber bites and store the toppings separately for up to 2 days.

CHICKPEA PATTIES WITH HARISSA YOGURT

PREP TIME: 15 MINUTES
DIETARY: GLUTEN-FREE, VEGETARIAN

210 CALORIES, 7G PROTEIN, 22G CARBS, 11G FAT

INGREDIENTS:

- 1 can (15 oz) chickpeas (drained and rinsed)
- 1 small onion (chopped)
- 2 tbsp chickpea flour (or regular flour)
- 1 clove garlic (minced)
- 1 tsp ground cumin
- 2 tbsp olive oil
- Salt and pepper to taste
- Harissa Yogurt:
- ¼ cup Greek yogurt
- 1 tsp harissa paste (adjust to taste)
- Salt and pepper to taste

INSTRUCTIONS:

1. In a food processor, pulse the chickpeas, onion, garlic, cumin, flour, salt, and pepper until a rough mixture forms.
2. Shape the mixture into small patties.
3. Heat olive oil in a skillet over medium heat. Cook the patties for 3-4 minutes on each side until golden brown.
4. Mix the harissa and yogurt together.
5. Serve the chickpea patties with harissa yogurt.

BATCH-COOKING TIP: Make extra chickpea patties and store them in the fridge for up to 3 days. Reheat them in the oven or skillet.

TREATS

ALMOND AND ORANGE BLOSSOM COOKIES

PREP TIME: 15 MINUTES
DIETARY: GLUTEN-FREE, DAIRY-FREE, VEGAN

150 CALORIES, 3G PROTEIN, 15G CARBS, 9G FAT

INGREDIENTS:

- 1 cup almond flour
- 2 tbsp honey (or maple syrup for vegan)
- 1 tbsp orange blossom water
- 1 tbsp olive oil
- 1 tsp baking powder
- 1 tsp vanilla extract
- Pinch of salt

INSTRUCTIONS:

1. Preheat the oven to 350°F (180°C).
2. In a bowl, combine the almond flour, honey, orange blossom water, olive oil, baking powder, vanilla extract, and salt. Mix until a dough forms.
3. Scoop tablespoon-sized portions of dough and roll into balls. Flatten slightly on a baking sheet lined with parchment paper.
4. Bake for 8-10 minutes, until golden brown. Let cool before serving.

BATCH-COOKING TIP: Make extra cookies and store them in an airtight container for up to a week.

GREEK YOGURT WITH HONEY AND WALNUTS

PREP TIME: 5 MINUTES
DIETARY: GLUTEN-FREE, VEGETARIAN

180 CALORIES, 8G PROTEIN, 20G CARBS, 7G FAT

INGREDIENTS:

- 1 cup Greek yogurt
- 2 tbsp honey
- 2 tbsp walnuts (chopped)

- ½ tsp cinnamon (optional)

INSTRUCTIONS:

5. Divide the Greek yogurt between two bowls.
6. Drizzle with honey and sprinkle with chopped walnuts.
7. Optionally, dust with cinnamon before serving.

BATCH-COOKING TIP: Make extra servings and store in the fridge for up to 2 days. Stir just before serving for freshness.

TAHINI AND DATE BLISS BALLS

PREP TIME: 10 MINUTES
DIETARY: GLUTEN-FREE, DAIRY-FREE, VEGAN

130 CALORIES, 3G PROTEIN, 16G CARBS, 6G FAT

INGREDIENTS:

- 1 cup pitted dates
- 2 tbsp tahini
- ¼ cup oats (gluten-free if necessary)
- 1 tbsp cocoa powder
- 2 tbsp shredded coconut (optional)

INSTRUCTIONS:

1. In a food processor, combine the dates, tahini, oats, and cocoa powder. Blend until the mixture comes together into a sticky dough.
2. Roll the mixture into tablespoon-sized balls.
3. Roll each ball in shredded coconut (optional) for

extra texture.
4. Chill in the fridge for 15 minutes before serving.

BATCH-COOKING TIP: Make extra bliss balls and store them in the fridge for up to a week. Perfect for a quick snack or dessert.

OLIVE OIL AND LEMON CAKE BITES

PREP TIME: 15 MINUTES
DIETARY: DAIRY-FREE, VEGETARIAN

190 CALORIES, 4G PROTEIN, 24G CARBS, 8G FAT

INGREDIENTS:

- ½ cup all-purpose flour (or gluten-free flour)
- ¼ cup olive oil
- ¼ cup sugar
- 1 egg
- Zest of 1 lemon
- 1 tsp baking powder
- Pinch of salt

INSTRUCTIONS:

1. Preheat the oven to 350°F (180°C).
2. In a bowl, whisk together the olive oil, sugar, and egg. Add the flour, lemon zest, baking powder, and salt, and mix until smooth.
3. Pour the batter into a greased mini muffin tin.
4. Bake for 10-12 minutes until golden and set. Let cool before serving.

BATCH-COOKING TIP: Make extra cake bites and store them in an airtight container for up to 3 days.

HONEY AND PISTACHIO BAKLAVA CUPS

PREP TIME: 10 MINUTES
DIETARY: VEGETARIAN

210 CALORIES, 4G PROTEIN, 25G CARBS, 11G FAT

INGREDIENTS:

- 6 sheets of phyllo dough (cut into squares)
- ½ cup pistachios (chopped)
- 2 tbsp honey

1 tbsp melted butter (or olive oil for dairy-free)
1 tsp cinnamon

INSTRUCTIONS:

1. Preheat the oven to 350°F (180°C).
2. Brush each phyllo square with melted butter and layer 3 squares into each cup of a mini muffin tin.
3. In a bowl, mix the chopped pistachios, honey, and cinnamon. Spoon the mixture into each phyllo cup.
4. Bake for 8-10 minutes, until the edges are golden and crisp. Serve warm or at room temperature.

BATCH-COOKING TIP: Make extra baklava cups and store them at room temperature for up to 2 days.

FIG AND ALMOND BARS

PREP TIME: 10 MINUTES
DIETARY: GLUTEN-FREE, DAIRY-FREE, VEGAN

0 CALORIES, 4G PROTEIN, 20G CARBS, 8G FAT

INGREDIENTS:

- 1 cup dried figs (chopped)
- ½ cup almond flour
- ¼ cup oats (gluten-free if necessary)
- 2 tbsp maple syrup or honey
- 1 tbsp almond butter
- ½ tsp cinnamon

INSTRUCTIONS:

1. Preheat the oven to 350°F (180°C).
2. In a bowl, combine the chopped figs, almond flour, oats, maple syrup, almond butter, and cinnamon. Mix until it forms a sticky dough.
3. Press the mixture into a greased or lined 8x8 inch baking pan.
4. Bake for 10-12 minutes until lightly golden. Let cool, then cut into bars before serving.

BATCH-COOKING TIP: Make extra bars and store them in an airtight container for up to 4 days.

POMEGRANATE AND ROSEWATER SORBET

PREP TIME: 5 MINUTES + 15 MINUTES FREEZE TIME
DIETARY: GLUTEN-FREE, DAIRY-FREE, VEGAN

110 CALORIES, 1G PROTEIN, 25G CARBS, 0G FAT

INGREDIENTS:

- 2 cups pomegranate juice
- 1 tbsp rosewater
- 2 tbsp sugar or honey
- Fresh pomegranate seeds for garnish

INSTRUCTIONS:

5. In a bowl, whisk together the pomegranate juice, rosewater, and sugar until the sugar dissolves.
6. Pour the mixture into an ice cube tray or shallow pan and freeze for 15-20 minutes, scraping with a fork every 5 minutes until it forms a slushy texture.
7. Scoop into bowls and garnish with fresh pomegranate seeds.

BATCH-COOKING TIP: Make extra sorbet and store it in the freezer for up to 1 week. Scrape and serve as needed.

RICOTTA WITH BERRIES AND BALSAMIC GLAZE

PREP TIME: 5 MINUTES
DIETARY: GLUTEN-FREE, VEGETARIAN

190 CALORIES, 7G PROTEIN, 15G CARBS, 10G FAT

INGREDIENTS:

- 1 cup ricotta cheese
- ½ cup mixed berries (strawberries, raspberries, blueberries)
- 1 tbsp balsamic glaze
- 1 tbsp honey (optional)

INSTRUCTIONS:

1. Spoon the ricotta cheese into bowls.
2. Top with mixed berries, drizzle with balsamic glaze, and honey (if using).
3. Serve immediately for a fresh, light dessert.

BATCH-COOKING TIP: Store extra ricotta and berries separately in the fridge for up to 2 days. Assemble just before serving.

QUICK CINNAMON-SUGAR PITA CHIPS WITH YOGURT DIP

PREP TIME: 5 MINUTES
COOK TIME: 10 MINUTES
DIETARY: VEGETARIAN

180 CALORIES, 5G PROTEIN, 25G CARBS, 6G FAT

INGREDIENTS:

- 2 pita breads (cut into triangles)
- 2 tbsp olive oil
- 2 tbsp sugar
- 1 tsp cinnamon
- Yogurt Dip:
- ½ cup Greek yogurt
- 1 tsp honey
- ½ tsp vanilla extract

INSTRUCTIONS:

1. Preheat the oven to 375°F (190°C).
2. Brush the pita triangles with olive oil and sprinkle with cinnamon and sugar.
3. Bake for 8-10 minutes until crispy and golden.
4. Mix the Greek yogurt, honey, and vanilla extract in a bowl for the dip.
5. Serve the pita chips with the yogurt dip.

BATCH-COOKING TIP:
Store extra pita chips in an airtight container for up to 3 days

ORANGE SEMOLINA CAKE

PREP TIME: 15 MINUTES
DIETARY: DAIRY-FREE, VEGETARIAN

220 CALORIES, 4G PROTEIN, 30G CARBS, 10G FAT

INGREDIENTS:

- 1 cup semolina flour
- ½ cup orange juice
- ¼ cup olive oil
- ½ cup sugar
- Zest of 1 orange
- 1 tsp baking powder

INSTRUCTIONS:

1. Preheat the oven to 350°F (180°C).
2. In a bowl, mix the semolina flour, orange juice, olive oil, sugar, orange zest, and baking powder until smooth.
3. Pour the batter into a greased loaf pan.
4. Bake for 10-12 minutes until set and golden. Serve warm or at room temperature.

BATCH-COOKING TIP: Make extra cake and store it in an airtight container for up to 3 days.

SESAME HALVA WITH CHOCOLATE DRIZZLE

PREP TIME: 15 MINUTES
DIETARY: GLUTEN-FREE, DAIRY-FREE, VEGAN

200 CALORIES, 5G PROTEIN, 15G CARBS, 12G FAT

INGREDIENTS:

- ½ cup tahini
- ¼ cup honey or maple syrup
- 2 tbsp sesame seeds (toasted)
- 1 tbsp cocoa powder
- ¼ cup dark chocolate (melted, for drizzle)

INSTRUCTIONS:

1. In a bowl, mix together the tahini, honey, sesame seeds, and cocoa powder until well combined.
2. Spread the mixture into a small, lined container or pan, smoothing it out.
3. Drizzle the melted dark chocolate over the top.
4. Chill in the fridge for 10 minutes until firm. Cut into squares before serving.

BATCH-COOKING TIP: Make extra halva and store it in the fridge for up to 5 days. Serve chilled or at room temperature.

COCONUT DATE ROLLS WITH ALMONDS

PREP TIME: 5 MINUTES
DIETARY: GLUTEN-FREE, DAIRY-FREE, VEGAN

150 CALORIES, 3G PROTEIN, 18G CARBS, 8G FAT

INGREDIENTS:

- 1 cup pitted dates
- ¼ cup shredded coconut
- ¼ cup almonds (chopped)
- 1 tbsp almond butter

INSTRUCTIONS:

1. In a food processor, blend the pitted dates and almond butter until smooth.
2. Roll the mixture into small balls, then coat them in shredded coconut and chopped almonds.
3. Chill in the fridge for 15 minutes before serving.

BATCH-COOKING TIP: Make extra rolls and store them in the fridge for up to a week. Great for a quick snack or dessert.

DRESSINGS & SAUCES

TAHINI LEMON DRESSING

PREP TIME: 5 MINUTES
DIETARY: GLUTEN-FREE, VEGAN

INGREDIENTS:
- ¼ cup tahini
- Juice of 1 lemon
- 1 clove garlic (minced)
- 2 tbsp olive oil
- 2-3 tbsp water (to thin)
- ½ tsp ground cumin
- Salt and pepper to taste

INSTRUCTIONS:
1. In a small bowl, whisk together the tahini, lemon juice, and minced garlic until smooth.
2. Slowly whisk in the olive oil and cumin, adding water 1 tablespoon at a time until you reach your desired consistency.
3. Season with salt and pepper to taste. The dressing should be creamy but pourable.

STORAGE TIPS:
In the Fridge: Store the tahini lemon dressing in an airtight container for up to 1 week. If it thickens in the fridge, whisk in a bit of water or lemon juice to bring it back to the right consistency.

Freezing Tahini Dressing: Tahini-based dressings can be frozen, but the texture may separate. Freeze in an airtight container for up to 1 month. Thaw in the fridge overnight and whisk well before using.

HOW TO USE TAHINI LEMON DRESSING:
Salad Dressing: Drizzle over green salads or grain bowls for a creamy, tangy flavor.

Dip: Serve as a dip for roasted vegetables, pita, or falafel.

Sauce for Roasted Vegetables: Use it as a topping for roasted or grilled vegetables.

Sandwich Spread: Spread it inside wraps or sandwiches for a tangy, creamy element.

CLASSIC GREEK VINAIGRETTE

PREP TIME: 5 MINUTES
DIETARY: GLUTEN-FREE, DAIRY-FREE, VEGAN

INGREDIENTS:
- ¼ cup extra virgin olive oil
- 2 tbsp red wine vinegar
- 1 tsp Dijon mustard
- 1 clove garlic (minced)
- 1 tsp dried oregano
- Salt and pepper to taste

INSTRUCTIONS:
1. In a small bowl, whisk together the olive oil, red wine vinegar, Dijon mustard, and minced garlic until emulsified.
2. Stir in the dried oregano, and season with salt and pepper to taste.

STORAGE TIPS:

In the Fridge: This vinaigrette can be stored in the refrigerator for up to 2 weeks. If the oil solidifies in the fridge, allow it to sit at room temperature for a few minutes before use and shake or whisk to recombine.

Freezing Vinaigrette: Freezing is not recommended for vinaigrettes, as the oil may separate and affect the texture when thawed.

HOW TO USE CLASSIC GREEK VINAIGRETTE:

Salad Dressing: Toss with fresh greens, cucumbers, tomatoes, and olives for a Greek salad.

Marinade: Use as a marinade for chicken, shrimp, or tofu before grilling.

Drizzle Over Grains: Pour over cooked grains like quinoa or bulgur for extra flavor.

Vegetable Topping: Drizzle over roasted or grilled vegetables to add a tangy finish.

TZATZIKI SAUCE

PREP TIME: 10 MINUTES
DIETARY: GLUTEN-FREE, CAN BE MADE VEGAN WITH DAIRY-FREE YOGURT

INGREDIENTS:

1 cup Greek yogurt (or dairy-free yogurt for a vegan option)
½ cucumber (grated and drained)
1 clove garlic (minced)
1 tbsp olive oil
1 tbsp fresh dill (chopped)
Juice of ½ lemon
Salt and pepper to taste

INSTRUCTIONS:

1. In a medium bowl, combine the yogurt, grated cucumber (squeeze out excess water), minced garlic, olive oil, dill, and lemon juice.
2. Stir until well combined, and season with salt and pepper to taste.

STORAGE TIPS:

In the Fridge: Store tzatziki in an airtight container in the refrigerator for up to 4 days. Stir before each use as the cucumber may release water over time.

Freezing Tzatziki: Freezing is not recommended as the texture of the cucumber and yogurt may become watery when thawed.

HOW TO USE TZATZIKI SAUCE:

Dip: Serve with pita, vegetables, or as part of a mezze platter.

Sauce for Grilled Meats: Use it as a sauce for grilled chicken, lamb, or kebabs.

Spread: Spread it on wraps or sandwiches for a refreshing, creamy element.

Salad Dressing: Thin with a bit of water and use it as a light salad dressing.

HARISSA SAUCE

PREP TIME: 5 MINUTES
DIETARY: GLUTEN-FREE, DAIRY-FREE, VEGAN

INGREDIENTS:

- 3 tbsp harissa paste (store-bought or homemade)
- 1 tbsp olive oil
- Juice of ½ lemon
- 1 clove garlic (minced)
- ½ tsp ground cumin
- ¼ cup water (to thin)

INSTRUCTIONS:

1. In a bowl, mix together the harissa paste, olive oil, lemon juice, minced garlic, cumin, and water until smooth.
2. Adjust the consistency with more water if needed. The sauce should be pourable but thick.

STORAGE TIPS:

In the Fridge: Store harissa sauce in an airtight container for up to 1 week. Stir well before use as it may thicken over time.

Freezing Harissa Sauce: Harissa sauce freezes well for up to 2 months. Thaw overnight in the fridge and stir before use.

HOW TO USE HARISSA SAUCE:

Drizzle Over Roasted Vegetables: Use it as a spicy sauce for roasted vegetables like carrots, cauliflower, or potatoes.

Add to Grains: Mix with quinoa, couscous, or rice for a flavorful side dish.

Sauce for Grilled Meats: Serve it with grilled chicken, beef, or lamb kebabs for a spicy kick.

Use in Wraps: Spread it inside wraps with falafel, chicken, or roasted veggies for extra heat and flavor.

LABNEH

PREP TIME: 10 MINUTES (PLUS 24-48 HOURS FOR STRAINING)
DIETARY: GLUTEN-FREE, CAN BE MADE VEGAN

INGREDIENTS:

- 2 cups full-fat Greek yogurt (or use dairy-free yogurt for a vegan option)
- 1 tsp salt
- Cheesecloth (or a clean kitchen towel)
- A fine mesh strainer
- A bowl for draining

INSTRUCTIONS:

1. In a bowl, mix the Greek yogurt with salt until fully combined.
2. Place a fine mesh strainer over a large bowl and line it with a cheesecloth or clean kitchen towel.
3. Pour the yogurt mixture into the cloth, then bring the edges of the cloth together and tie it up securely.
4. Let the yogurt strain in the fridge for 24-48 hours, depending on how thick you want the labneh. The longer it strains, the thicker and creamier it will become.
5. After the straining time is up, transfer the thickened labneh to an airtight container and refrigerate.

STORAGE TIPS:

In the Fridge: Labneh can be stored in an airtight container in the refrigerator for up to 2 weeks.

Preserving in Olive Oil: For longer storage and added flavor, roll the labneh into small balls and place them in a jar covered with olive oil. This can extend its freshness for up to a month.

Freezing Labneh: Labneh can also be frozen, but freezing might change its texture slightly. To freeze, place in an airtight container for up to 2 months. Thaw overnight in the fridge and stir well before use.

HOW TO USE LABNEH:

Spread on Toast: Use labneh as a spread on bread or crackers.

As a Dip: Serve it as a dip with pita, vegetables, or as part of a mezze platter.

In Sandwiches: Use labneh instead of mayo or other spreads for a tangy, creamy texture.

Topping: Add it as a creamy topping for roasted vegetables, grilled meats, or soups.

GARLIC AIOLI

PREP TIME: 5 MINUTES
DIETARY: GLUTEN-FREE, DAIRY-FREE, CAN BE MADE VEGAN

INGREDIENTS:

- ½ cup mayonnaise (or vegan mayo for a plant-based option)
- 2 cloves garlic (minced)
- 1 tbsp lemon juice
- 1 tsp Dijon mustard
- Salt and pepper to taste

INSTRUCTIONS:

1. In a small bowl, combine the mayonnaise, minced garlic, lemon juice, and Dijon mustard.
2. Whisk until smooth and creamy. Season with salt and pepper to taste.

STORAGE TIPS:

In the Fridge: Store garlic aioli in an airtight container for up to 5 days. Stir well before each use.

Freezing Aioli: Freezing is not recommended as mayonnaise-based sauces may separate when thawed.

HOW TO USE GARLIC AIOLI:

As a Dip: Serve with roasted vegetables, fries, or pita bread.

Spread for Sandwiches: Use as a flavorful spread in sandwiches and wraps.

Sauce for Grilled Meats: Serve alongside grilled chicken, fish, or steak for a creamy garlic kick.

Topping for Burgers: Add a spoonful on top of burgers or veggie patties for extra flavor.

BASIL PESTO

PREP TIME: 5 MINUTES
DIETARY: GLUTEN-FREE, VEGETARIAN (VEGAN OPTION WITH DAIRY-FREE CHEESE)

INGREDIENTS:

- 2 cups fresh basil leaves
- ¼ cup Parmesan cheese (or dairy-free alternative)
- ¼ cup pine nuts (or walnuts)
- 2 cloves garlic
- ½ cup olive oil
- Juice of ½ lemon
- Salt and pepper to taste

INSTRUCTIONS:

1. In a food processor, combine the basil, Parmesan cheese, pine nuts, garlic, and lemon juice.
2. Slowly drizzle in the olive oil while blending until smooth.
3. Season with salt and pepper to taste.

STORAGE TIPS:

In the Fridge: Store pesto in an airtight container for up to 1 week. To prevent browning, cover the surface with a thin layer of olive oil.

Freezing Pesto: Freeze pesto in small portions (ice cube trays work great) for up to 3 months. Thaw overnight in the fridge and stir before using.

HOW TO USE BASIL PESTO:

Toss with Pasta: Mix with your favorite pasta or zucchini noodles.

Spread on Sandwiches: Use it as a flavorful spread for sandwiches or wraps.

Topping for Grilled Meats: Drizzle over grilled chicken, fish, or tofu.

Sauce for Veggies: Use as a sauce for roasted vegetables or mixed into salads.

ROMESCO SAUCE

PREP TIME: 10 MINUTES
DIETARY: GLUTEN-FREE, DAIRY-FREE, VEGAN

INGREDIENTS:

- 1 jar (12 oz) roasted red peppers (drained)
- ½ cup almonds (toasted)
- 1 clove garlic
- 1 tbsp red wine vinegar
- ¼ cup olive oil
- 1 tsp smoked paprika
- Salt and pepper to taste

INSTRUCTIONS:

1. In a food processor, combine the roasted red peppers, toasted almonds, garlic, red wine vinegar, and smoked paprika.
2. Blend while slowly drizzling in the olive oil until smooth.
3. Season with salt and pepper to taste.

STORAGE TIPS:

In the Fridge: Store Romesco sauce in an airtight container for up to 1 week.

Freezing Romesco: Romesco sauce freezes well for up to 2 months. Thaw overnight in the fridge and stir before using.

HOW TO USE ROMESCO SAUCE:

Sauce for Grilled Vegetables: Serve with roasted or grilled veggies for a smoky flavor.

Spread for Sandwiches: Add to sandwiches or wraps as a zesty spread.

Drizzle Over Grains: Pour over cooked quinoa, couscous, or rice bowls.

Serve with Grilled Meats: Use as a sauce for grilled chicken, fish, or pork.

CUCUMBER-YOGURT SAUCE

PREP TIME: 5 MINUTES
DIETARY: GLUTEN-FREE, VEGETARIAN, CAN BE MADE VEGAN WITH DAIRY-FREE YOGURT

INGREDIENTS:

- 1 cup Greek yogurt (or dairy-free yogurt)
- ½ cucumber (grated and drained)
- 1 clove garlic (minced)
- 1 tbsp fresh dill (chopped)
- Juice of ½ lemon
- Salt and pepper to taste

INSTRUCTIONS:

1. In a bowl, combine the Greek yogurt, grated cucumber (squeeze out excess water), garlic, dill, and lemon juice.
2. Stir until smooth, and season with salt and pepper to taste.

STORAGE TIPS:

In the Fridge: Store in an airtight container for up to 3 days. Stir before each use as the cucumber may release water over time.

Freezing is not recommended as the yogurt may become watery when thawed.

HOW TO USE CUCUMBER-YOGURT SAUCE:

As a Dip: Serve with raw vegetables, pita, or falafel.

Topping for Grilled Meats: Use it as a cooling sauce for grilled chicken, lamb, or kebabs.

Spread for Sandwiches: Spread on wraps or pita for a fresh and tangy flavor.

Salad Dressing: Thin with a bit of water and use as a light dressing for salads.

CHIMICHURRI SAUCE

PREP TIME: 5 MINUTES
DIETARY: GLUTEN-FREE, DAIRY-FREE, VEGAN

INGREDIENTS:

- 1 cup fresh parsley (chopped)
- ½ cup fresh cilantro (chopped)
- 2 cloves garlic (minced)
- ½ tsp red pepper flakes
- ¼ cup olive oil
- 2 tbsp red wine vinegar
- Salt and pepper to taste

INSTRUCTIONS:

1. In a small bowl, whisk together the parsley, cilantro, garlic, red pepper flakes, olive oil, and red wine vinegar.
2. Season with salt and pepper to taste. Adjust the consistency by adding more olive oil if needed.

STORAGE TIPS:

In the Fridge: Store chimichurri in an airtight container for up to 1 week. Stir before use.

Freezing Chimichurri: Freeze in small portions for up to 2 months. Thaw in the fridge and stir before using.

HOW TO USE CHIMICHURRI SAUCE:

Sauce for Grilled Meats: Drizzle over grilled steak, chicken, or pork.

Topping for Vegetables: Use as a sauce for roasted or grilled vegetables.

Spread for Sandwiches: Add to sandwiches or wraps for a fresh, herby kick.

Drizzle Over Eggs: Use it as a topping for scrambled or fried eggs for extra flavor.

MEAL PLAN FOR COUPLES

This couple's meal plan is designed to simplify healthy eating by offering a single meal plan that works for both partners. Each day is calculated to provide 1200/1300 calories, ideal for women aiming for weight loss. For men, or those needing additional calories, the plan includes easy add-ons that bring meals up to 1,700/1,800 calories, making it perfect for men pursuing weight loss. This approach not only supports balanced nutrition and individual calorie goals but also eliminates the hassle of cooking separate meals!

WHY THESE CALORIE INTAKES WERE CHOSEN

The selected calorie ranges are based on general guidelines for safe and sustainable weight loss. Consuming fewer calories than your body expends leads to weight loss. However, it's important to avoid excessively low calorie intake, which can lead to nutrient deficiencies and decreased energy levels. The provided calorie ranges aim to create a moderate calorie deficit while maintaining nutritional balance.

MEAL PREP SUGGESTIONS

Efficient meal preparation is key to staying on track with your dietary goals. Here are some tips to help you manage your time and make meal prep more enjoyable:

- **Weekly Planning:** Review the meal plan at the beginning of each week. Take note of recipes that can be prepared in larger batches and reused, such as soups, stews, and grain dishes.
- **Batch Cooking:** Cook larger quantities of staple ingredients like quinoa, brown rice, grilled chicken, and roasted vegetables. These can be stored in the refrigerator and used in various meals throughout the week.
- **Utilize Leftovers:** Plan meals that can be repurposed. For example, leftover grilled chicken from dinner can be added to salads or wraps for lunch the next day.
- **Grocery Shopping:** Use the provided weekly shopping lists to streamline your grocery trips. Buying in bulk and choosing versatile ingredients saves time and money.
- **Freeze for Later:** Certain dishes like soups, stews, and sauces freeze well. Consider doubling recipes and freezing portions for future use.

- **Prep Ingredients:** Wash and chop vegetables ahead of time. Store them properly so they're ready when you need them, reducing meal prep time.

ADDITIONAL TIPS

- **Stay Hydrated:** Aim to drink at least 8 cups of water daily. Hydration is crucial for overall health and can aid in weight loss.
- **Listen to Your Body:** Pay attention to hunger and fullness cues. Adjust portion sizes if needed to meet your individual needs.
- **Physical Activity:** Incorporate regular exercise into your routine to enhance weight loss efforts and promote overall well-being.
- **Flexibility:** Feel free to swap meals within the same week to suit your preferences. The goal is to make the meal plan work for you.

A NOTE ON PERSONALIZATION

While this meal plan provides a structured approach to weight loss, individual calorie needs can vary based on factors like age, weight, height, activity level, and health status. It's recommended to consult a healthcare professional or registered dietitian to tailor the plan to your specific needs.

 SCAN THIS QR CODE TO DOWNLOAD AND PRINT YOUR SHOPPING LIST

Weight Lost Meal-Plan For Couples

WEEK 1	MONDAY	TUESDAY	WEDNSDAY	THURSDAY	FRIDAY	SATURDAY	SUNDAY
BREAKFAST	Greek Yogurt with Honey and Walnuts - Greek yogurt, honey, chopped walnuts. For Him: Add sliced banana and extra walnuts.	Overnight Oats with Berries and Honey - Rolled oats, almond milk, mixed berries, honey. For Him: Add chia seeds and extra oats.	Greek Yogurt with Honey and Walnuts - Repeat from Day 1. For Him: Add strawberries and extra honey.	Avocado Toast with Tomato - Whole-grain toast, mashed avocado, sliced tomato. For Him: Add 2 scrambled eggs.	Berry Smoothie Bowl - Blended berries, banana, almond milk, topped with granola. For Him: Add peanut butter and extra granola.	Overnight Oats with Berries and Honey - Repeat from Day 2. For Him: Add sliced almonds and extra honey.	Greek Yogurt with Honey and Walnuts - Repeat from previous days. For Him: Add granola and sliced banana.
LUNCH	Grilled Lemon-Herb Chicken with Olive & Cucumber Salad - Recipe #1. For Him: Include whole-wheat pita bread.	Mediterranean Tuna Salad with White Beans - Recipe #9, over mixed greens. For Him: Include whole-grain bread	Vegetarian Stuffed Peppers with Quinoa & Feta - Recipe #5. For Him: Add extra pepper half and hummus with veggies.	Quick Mediterranean Pasta with Olives, Capers & Cherry Tomatoes - Recipe #3. For Him: Increase pasta and add grilled chicken.	Mediterranean Lentil Salad with Feta & Herbs - Recipe #5 from the Salads For Him: Include whole-wheat pita and tzatziki.	Mediterranean Chicken Wrap with Hummus & Veggies - Recipe #19. For Him: Add extra chicken and baked sweet potato fries.	Mediterranean Veggie Frittata - Recipe #16, with mixed greens. For Him: Add whole-grain toast with avocado spread.
SNACK	Small apple with 1 tbsp almond butter.	Handful of mixed nuts (1 oz).	Carrot sticks with 2 tbsp hummus.	Small Greek yogurt with honey.	Sliced cucumber and bell peppers with hummus.	Pear with a small handful of walnuts.	Small smoothie with almond milk, spinach, and pineapple.
DINNER	One-Pot Lemon Orzo with Spinach & Chickpeas - Recipe #2. For Him: Increase portion and add side salad with olive oil dressing.	Garlic Shrimp with Lemon & Parsley - Recipe #10, with steamed broccoli and quinoa. For Him: Increase quinoa and add roasted sweet potatoes.	Quick Chicken Skewers with Garlic Yogurt Sauce - Recipe #27, with grilled zucchini. For Him: Add Mediterranean Spiced Rice. noa and add roasted sweet	Chickpea and Spinach Stew with Harissa - Recipe #11, over couscous. For Him: Increase couscous and add grilled halloumi.	Pan-Seared Salmon with Tomato & Olive Relish - Recipe #4, with steamed asparagus. For Him: Add Mediterranean Rice Pilaf.	Grilled Mahi-Mahi with Olive Tapenade - Recipe #25, served over quinoa. For Him: Increase quinoa and add side salad with olive oil dressing.	Grilled Chicken Shawarma with Tahini Sauce - Recipe #8, with roasted cauliflower. For Him: Add Mediterranean Spiced Rice.
KCAL	Her: ~1,200 Him: ~1,700	Her: ~1,270 Him: ~1,770	Her: ~1,140 Him: ~1,620	Her: ~1,200 Him: ~1,800	Her: ~1,190 Him: ~1,740	Her: ~1,260 Him: ~1,810	Her: ~1,140 Him: ~1,670

Weight Lost Meal-Plan For Couples

WEEK 2	MONDAY	TUESDAY	WEDNSDAY	THURSDAY	FRIDAY	SATURDAY	SUNDAY
BREAKFAST	Spinach and Feta Omelette - Eggs, spinach, feta cheese. For Him: Add whole-grain toast with avocado.	Overnight Chia Pudding with Berries - Chia seeds, almond milk, mixed berries. For Him: Add a banana and extra chia seeds.	Greek Yogurt with Honey and Walnuts - Repeat from Week 1 for easy prep. For Him: Add granola and sliced banana	Avocado and Tomato Whole-Grain Toast - Repeat from Week 1. For Him: Add a hard-boiled egg.	Berry Smoothie Bowl - Repeat from Week 1. For Him: Add almond butter and extra granola.	Spinach and Feta Omelette - Repeat from Day 8. For Him: Add whole-grain toast.	Greek Yogurt with Honey and Walnuts - Consistent breakfast for easy prep. For Him: Add sliced peaches and extra walnuts.
LUNCH	Creamy Roasted Red Pepper and White Bean Soup - Recipe #1 from Soups. For Him: Include a whole-grain roll.	Quinoa Tabbouleh Salad - Recipe #2 from Salads (substitute quinoa for bulgur). For Him: Include grilled chicken strips.	Mediterranean Veggie Wrap with Hummus - Whole-wheat wrap, hummus, cucumber, tomatoes, spinach. For Him: Add grilled chicken slices.	Mediterranean Chickpea Salad with Lemon and Herbs - Recipe #3 from Salads. For Him: Include whole-grain pita bread.	Roasted Vegetable and Quinoa Bowl - Roasted zucchini, eggplant, peppers over quinoa. For Him: Add grilled chicken.	Mediterranean Tuna Salad Lettuce Wraps - Lite Bites Recipe #14. For Him: Include a side of whole-grain crackers.	Eggplant and Zucchini Stir-Fry with Garlic and Herbs - Recipe #21, served over brown rice. For Him: Add grilled salmon.
SNACK	A small pear with a tablespoon of almond butter.	Handful of mixed nuts (1 oz).	Carrot sticks with 2 tbsp tzatziki.	Small Greek yogurt with honey and berries.	Sliced apple with 1 tbsp peanut butter.	Cucumber slices with hummus.	Small smoothie with almond milk, spinach, and mango.
DINNER	Grilled Turkey Kebabs with Cucumber Mint Salad - Recipe #30. For Him: Increase portion and add a side of Mediterranean Spiced Rice.	Pan-Seared Cod with Tomato-Caper Salsa - Recipe #16. For Him: Add roasted sweet potatoes.	Spaghetti Aglio e Olio with Spinach - Recipe #28. For Him: Increase pasta portion and add grilled shrimp.	Grilled Turkey Kebabs with Cucumber Mint Salad - Recipe #30. For Him: Increase kebab portions and add couscous.	Pan-Seared Chicken Thighs with Olives & Sundried Tomatoes - Recipe #24. For Him: Increase portion and add Mediterranean Rice Pilaf.	Moroccan Chicken Tagine with Apricots & Almonds - Recipe #31. For Him: Serve over couscous and increase portion.	Grilled Harissa Chicken Thighs with Herb Yogurt - Recipe #32. For Him: Increase portion and add roasted potatoes.
KCAL	Her: ~1,250 Him: ~1,750	Her: ~1,220 Him: ~1,720	Her: ~1,300 Him: ~1,800	Her: ~1,250 Him: ~1,750	Her: ~1,280 Him: ~1,780	Her: ~1,300 Him: ~1,800	Her: ~1,250 Him: ~1,750

Weight Lost Meal-Plan For Couples

WEEK 3	MONDAY	TUESDAY	WEDNSDAY	THURSDAY	FRIDAY	SATURDAY	SUNDAY
BREAKFAST	Oatmeal with Fresh Frui and Nuts - Rolled oats cooked with almond milk, topped with fresh berries and chopped almonds. For Him: Add a tablespoon of peanut butter and extra oats.	Greek Yogurt with Honey and Walnuts - Consistent breakfast for easy prep. For Him: Add granola and sliced banana.	Avocado and Tomato Whole-Grain Toast - Repeat from previous weeks. For Him: Add two scrambled eggs.	Berry Smoothie Bowl - Blended berries, spinach, almond milk, topped with sliced almonds. For Him: Add peanut butter and extra granola.	Overnight Oats with Berries and Honey - Repeat for easy prep. For Him: Add chia seeds and extra oats.	Spinach and Feta Omelette - Eggs, spinach, feta cheese. For Him: Add whole-grain toast with avocado.	Greek Yogurt with Honey and Walnuts - Consistent breakfast. For Him: Add sliced peaches and extra walnuts.
LUNCH	Quick Mediterranean Meatballs with Tzatziki - Recipe #22, served over mixed greens. For Him: Include whole-grain pita bread.	Spiced Lentil Patties with Harissa Yogurt - Recipe #32, served over a bed of spinach. For Him: Increase portion and add whole-wheat pita.	Chickpea Salad with Cucumber and Lemon - Salads Recipe #3. For Him: Include grilled chicken breast.	Mediterranean Chicken Wrap with Hummus & Veggies - Recipe #19. For Him: Add extra chicken and a side of baked sweet potato fries.	Greek Salad with Feta and Olives - Salads Recipe #1. For Him: Include grilled chicken strips.	Orzo Salad with Spinach and Sun-Dried Tomatoes - Salads Recipe #6. For Him: Add grilled shrimp.	Watermelon and Feta Salad with Mint - Salads Recipe #8. For Him: Include whole-grain roll and extra feta.
SNACK	Sliced bell peppers with hummus.	A small apple with almond butter.	Greek yogurt with berries.	Handful of mixed nuts (1 oz).	Carrot sticks with tzatziki.	Sliced cucumber with hummus.	Small smoothie with almond milk, spinach, and pineapple.
DINNER	Baked Cod with Tomato-Caper Salsa - Recipe #16, with steamed broccoli. For Him: Add a side of Mediterranean Spiced Rice.	Grilled Mahi-Mahi with Olive Tapenade - Recipe #25, with roasted asparagus. For Him: Add quinoa salad.	Quick Moroccan-Spiced Beef Skewers - Recipe #17, with grilled vegetables. For Him: Add couscous.	Eggplant & Zucchini Stir-Fry with Garlic and Pine Nuts - Recipe #2, over brown rice. For Him: Add grilled salmon.	Grilled Pork Chops with Mint Pesto - Recipe #20, with steamed green beans. For Him: Add roasted potatoes.	Quick Moroccan-Spiced Beef Skewers - Recipe #17, with couscous and roasted carrots. For Him: Increase portion size.	Pan-Seared Chicken Thighs with Olives & Sun-Dried Tomatoes - Recipe #31, with quinoa. For Him: Add side salad with olive oil dressing.
KCAL	Her: ~1,250 Him: ~1,750	Her: ~1,230 Him: ~1,730	Her: ~1,260 Him: ~1,760	Her: ~1,280 Him: ~1,780	Her: ~1,250 Him: ~1,750	Her: ~1,270 Him: ~1,770	Her: ~1,240 Him: ~1,740

Weight Lost Meal-Plan For Couples

WEEK 4	MONDAY	TUESDAY	WEDNSDAY	THURSDAY	FRIDAY	SATURDAY	SUNDAY
BREAKFAST	Greek Yogurt with Honey and Walnuts - Consistent breakfast for easy prep. For Him: Add sliced banana and extra walnuts.	Overnight Oats with Berries and Honey - Rolled oats, almond milk, mixed berries, honey. For Him: Add chia seeds and extra oats.	Spinach and Feta Omelette - Eggs, spinach, feta cheese. For Him: Add whole-grain toast with avocado.	Berry Smoothie Bowl - Blended berries, banana, almond milk, topped with granola. For Him: Add peanut butter and extra granola.	Avocado and Tomato Whole-Grain Toast - Whole-grain toast, mashed avocado, tomato slices. For Him: Add two scrambled eggs.	Greek Yogurt with Honey and Walnuts - Greek yogurt, honey, chopped walnuts. For Him: Add sliced peaches and extra walnuts.	Oatmeal with Fresh Fruit and Nuts - Rolled oats with almond milk, topped with berries and almonds. For Him: Add peanut butter and extra oats.
LUNCH	Mediterranean Veggie Frittata - Recipe #37, served with mixed greens. For Him: Include whole-grain toast with avocado spread.	Chickpea and Cucumber Salad with Lemon - Salads Recipe #3. For Him: Include grilled chicken breast.	Quinoa Tabbouleh Salad - Salads Recipe #2, using quinoa. For Him: Add grilled shrimp.	Creamy Roasted Red Pepper and White Bean Soup - Recipe #1 from Soups. For Him: Include a whole-grain roll.	Mediterranean Tuna Salad Lettuce Wraps - Lite Bites Recipe #14. For Him: Include whole-grain pita bread.	Orzo Salad with Spinach and Sun-Dried Tomatoes - Salads Recipe #6. For Him: Add grilled chicken strips.	Watermelon and Feta Salad with Mint - Salads Recipe #8. For Him: Include whole-grain roll and extra feta.
SNACK	Sliced apple with almond butter.	Handful of mixed nuts (1 oz).	Carrot sticks with 2 tbsp hummus.	Greek yogurt with a drizzle of honey.	Sliced cucumber with tzatziki.	Small smoothie with almond milk, spinach, and mango.	Sliced bell peppers with hummus.
DINNER	Grilled Shrimp Skewers with Lemon & Garlic - Recipe #10, served with quinoa and steamed broccoli. For Him: Increase shrimp portion and quinoa.	Grilled Turkey Kebabs with Cucumber Mint Salad - Recipe #30, with brown rice. For Him: Increase kebab portions and rice.	Pan-Seared Salmon with Tomato & Olive Relish - Recipe #22, with roasted asparagus. For Him: Add Mediterranean Spiced Rice.	Grilled Chicken Paillard with Arugula & Parmesan - Recipe #29, with roasted sweet potatoes. For Him: Increase chicken portion and sweet potatoes.	Moroccan Chicken Tagine with Apricots & Almonds - Recipe #31, over couscous. For Him: Increase portion size and couscous.	Grilled Harissa Chicken Thighs with Herb Yogurt - Recipe #32, with roasted vegetables. For Him: Add brown rice.	Grilled Mahi-Mahi with Olive Tapenade - Recipe #25, with quinoa and steamed broccoli. For Him: Increase fish portion and quinoa.
KCAL	Her: ~1,150 Him: ~1,680	Her: ~1,200 Him: ~1,750	Her: ~1,120 Him: ~1,720	Her: ~1,200 Him: ~1,750	Her: ~1,080 Him: ~1,680	Her: ~1,140 Him: ~1,690	Her: ~1,130 Him: ~1,680

Recipes Index

Conversion Chart

WEIGHT	
OUNCES	GRAMS
1/2	14
3/4	21
1	28
1 1/2	43
2	57
2 1/2	71
3	85
3 1/2	99
4	113
4 1/2	128
5	142
6	170
7	198
8	227
9	255
10	283
12	340
16 (1 pound)	454

TEMPERATURE	
FAHRENHEIT	CELSIUS
100	37
150	65
200	93
250	121
300	150
325	160
350	180
375	190
400	200
425	220
450	230
500	260
525	274
550	288

VOLUME	
U.S	METRIC
1 Teaspoon	5 ml
2 Teaspoons	10 ml
1 Tablespoon	15 ml
2 Tablespoons	30 ml
1/4 cup	59 ml
1/3 cup	79 ml
1/2 cup	118 ml
3/4 cup	177 ml
1 cup	237 ml
1 1/4 cup	296 ml
1 1/2 cup	355 ml
1 3/4 cup	414 ml
2 cups (1 pint) cup	473 ml
2 1/2 cup	591 ml
3 cup	255
4 (1 quart)	710 ml
1.06 quarts	1 liter ml

BONUS MATERIAL

28-DAY MEDITERRANEAN CHALLENGE
A checklist that encourages you to incorporate Mediterranean
lifestyle habits over 30 days

MEDITERRANEAN INGREDIENT SUBSTITUTION GUIDE
A handy guide for substituting expensive or hard-to-find
ingredients with more accessible or budget-friendly options.

PORTION CONTROL VISUAL GUIDE
A visual reference showing appropriate portion sizes for different
food groups, making it easier for readers to balance their meals.

 SCAN THIS QR CODE TO ACCESS
YOUR BONUSES

Made in United States
Orlando, FL
13 December 2024

55584301R00046